The Mountain

Andrassy út, Volume 2

David Antonelli

Published by David Antonelli, 2013.

While every precaution has been taken in the preparation of this book, the publisher assumes no responsibility for errors or omissions, or for damages resulting from the use of the information contained herein.

THE MOUNTAIN

First edition. May 25, 2013.

Copyright © 2013 David Antonelli.

ISBN: 979-8224198986

Written by David Antonelli.

Part I

I

The lights of the clay-tiled boardwalk flared and sputtered as the sun dropped below the horizon, casting brilliant bronze reflections off the shop windows, these myriad forms slowly vanishing into the warm lantern glow from inside the empty Austrian style cafés before finally giving way to the evening life of the village. A few young women stood on the street corner as though waiting for an intimate acquaintance to pick them up and take them to some restaurant or café. John Anderson watched them for a moment before closing his eyes and pressing his lips together. Something inside him told him *it was happening again*. He savored the words as though they were part of the opening titles of some great film that had just started playing in his head. What was happening again, he wasn't sure. This phrase had echoed inside him off and on through the course of his life, emerging in his mind like a momentary smile from an unknown woman suddenly vanishing behind the veil of an indifferent crowd, a labyrinth of memories and lost desire. It was an experience that always made him feel that something in his life was about to change in a chaotic and unforeseeable way, that now matter how jarring or even painful would ultimately guide him to a higher level of self awareness and understanding. He closed his eyes for an instant, shutting out the disturbances from the outside world. When he opened them again he parted the curtains and looked out the window. An old man crossed the small stone bridge that straddled the narrow brook passing through the park in front of Anderson's house and then flowing onwards towards the west side of the small shopping area that functioned as the center of the village. A child shouted something from across the street as he mounted his dark green bicycle; there was a loud crack like a firecracker and his voice was engulfed by the roar of a car from somewhere in the outskirts, Anderson couldn't tell where.

It was only the day before that he first learned of Anna's yearlong affair with a French diplomat. To make matters worse, an hour after his wife's confession news blared over the radio of Serbian troops thirty miles to the south advancing towards the village. Staying in Pozega any longer would be disastrous. Foreign journalists were stationed in or around Vukovar to the east, but that was too close to Serbia and with the onset of all-out war it was best to get out of Croatia altogether. A bridge five miles to the north had recently been bombed to cut off supply routes. If they could just avoid the main roads and villages and make it across that river and push as far as Velika at the foot of the Papuk Mountains they could evade the advancing troops for long enough to cross the mountains and make it to Barcs on the other side of the Hungarian border. As long as they had a good terrain map and stayed close enough to the roads for occasional navigation without being spotted they could make it safely without getting lost.

When Anna first told him about the affair he reacted in a way that even he found surprising. Instead of becoming angry with her, he took it as concrete indication of his failure to please her, something that he ultimately connected to his inability to find any lasting satisfaction in his professional life. "If a man can't please himself how can he please his wife?" he asked her as they edged slowly away from one another on the couch. Outside a dog barked nervously as though it had just confronted a foreign presence it neither trusted nor understood.

"I'm sorry," he said as he stood up to look out the window. Perhaps the dog was barking at an unseen intruder. When he turned back Anna had a look of hopelessness in her eyes that suggested she was disappointed in him, perhaps by the equanimity of his response. He wondered if it would have been better to get angry with her and slap her like many men he had seen do to their girlfriends in Yugoslavia. Yet for some reason he was not angry with her and couldn't deny that since moving to Yugoslavia to live out what they hoped would be their *Year of Living Dangerously*, with Anderson as Mel Gibson and Anna as Sigourney Weaver, their relationship had slowly dulled - the couple pried further and further apart by all of his commitments and the general malaise created by the Croatian War of Independence - to become little more than a series of borrowed events from other people's lives. In fact, nothing he had ever done laid any claim to being original. Even his most unique views or gestures could always be traced back to something his uncle or father might have said, echoed through his personal experiences and then hybridized by a few random ideas absorbed from yet another external source. Even his feeling that he should have slapped her instead of showing such magnanimity was based on what he had seen other men do rather than something that came from some deep inner conviction.

He hadn't spoken to Anna since this revelation and now there was the cataclysm of war to deal with. Anderson moved away from the window, determined to finally shout out something that was truly his own. Instead, he walked directly into the bedroom where she lay sleeping. He shook her warm and heavy form. She opened her eyes. They were deep and swollen like those of a child who had only minutes before cried her self to sleep.

"I'm not enough for you," he said. "I want you to leave now and start your life with someone else. It's the least we can do for each other."

She sighed and pressed her lips together in an expression of determination. "I think I need some orange juice," she said. Anderson's expression darkened. There were yellow stains the size of fingerprints spreading out from the middle of her pillow. Together they made a pattern like a faded map of imaginary countries from an equally imaginary world.

She turned and looked at him, her eyes suddenly more serious. "Look. I'm confused now. I was obviously confused then. Just give me some time. You know I can't imagine life without you."

"I should have loved you less. Or maybe I should have loved you more. Maybe there's no difference."

"Maybe there isn't," she said in a way that made him feel that she was right and that people always found different ways of loving one another and that affairs were just one of many such possibilities. He looked out the window at a man who was carrying a small child in the manner of a fire log as he walked in short urgent steps across the street.

"We have to get out of here," he said. "I don't think it's safe here anymore." He thought of the advancing troops and the prison camps at Velepromet and suddenly the affair seemed like a trivial episode from some television sitcom. She took his hand and squeezed it to signify that she was still his forever, or at least as long as it took to escape and start over somewhere else.

"When do we go?" was all she said. Anderson didn't answer. He was already too busy thinking about what they would do next and what was the best way to get to Barcs.

He stood up and walked in back to the living room. He looked once again through the windowpane, divided into six small squares by three crossed strips of lead, and now the man and child were both kneeling as they fed a few pigeons on the street below. *It was happening again*. That much he could hold onto. That much made him feel secure. Perhaps it was the sense of exhilaration at taking on the impossible, of having to save his marriage while at the same time potentially saving her life, that had temporarily suppressed his most negative feelings concerning her infidelity. Whatever it was, he was now a man who was sure of only two things: he and Anna were crossing the mountain to Hungary the very next morning and her affair was over.

When he returned to the bedroom Anna was asleep again, her soft white cheeks pressed up against her pillow. In the diffuse light of the candle burning beside her, she looked like a creature incapable of deceiving anyone. He resisted the urge to kiss her and slipped between the sheets beside her. In minutes he was asleep.

Anderson studied journalism at Columbia after taking an undergraduate degree in Classics and Modern Philosophy at a small liberal arts college in Pennsylvania. After his second year, he left New York to spend a year abroad working as a foreign writer on an English-speaking newspaper in Zurich in order to complete a practical requirement for his degree. He met Anna one April morning on a train from Zurich to Geneva. She was wearing a red summer dress and he immediately noticed her smooth forehead and straight brown hair, parted in the middle and falling to her shoulders. Her eyes were large and brown and very slightly angled in a way that gave the impression she was always just about to say something profound – it was a trait he would later suspect she used to gain power over other people, especially men, and perhaps even him. After an awkward conversation from across the aisle, frequently interrupted by a smug uniformed concierge who kept pushing a cart up and down the length of the train to offer the passengers drinks nobody seemed to want, he asked her if she could meet him for an early dinner somewhere in Geneva. She accepted and later that evening met at a restaurant near the train station that was known to the locals as one that only Americans would go to. She showed up in a light blue skirt and blouse, a trace of perfume lingering around her neck. That night they closed down the restaurant, only one dim light remaining on as they walked out into the crisp Swiss night. Anna seemed like the perfect woman for him. She was a relaxed but serious girl from wealthy merchant family in Great Falls, Montana. She had studied violin in New York before going to Prague for a few months to work as a waitress and take a break from any further studies. A few months after their first date he went back to New York and wrote her a letter inviting her to spend the summer with him. She accepted his invitation and they got married six months later.

What he had always craved for in her presence was exactly what he believed he was lacking. She would spend long reflective afternoons practicing violin while he read in the adjoining room in their cramped and modestly furnished New York apartment in Tribeca. She seemed perfectly comfortable just being in the world as a person with no special attachments or duties to fulfill. In this sense she was his opposite. She was always Anna as Anna and not Anna as the violinist, or Anna as the woman taking a six month hiatus from her studies or Anna the woman with the flower in her hair crossing the street when rain was threatening on a bright spring morning. It was this wholeness of being that drew him to her in the first place and this quality that had always kept him so close to her. Yet in her affair with the French diplomat – a man he had never met but for some reason imagined to have a short brushy mustache and spend long Sunday afternoons in Paris drinking exotic teas and listening to Edith Piaf – had something inside her changed to set this equilibrium off in some new and treacherous direction? He had always feared that one day she would grow tired of his restlessness and find someone new, someone more like herself. What was particularly disturbing was that he was completely unaware of her infidelity until she finally made her confession. And by that time it had long since been over. The entire affair – no doubt a vast brush-stroked fleshy canvas of five star hotels, Dom Perignon and fresh, perfumed linen - came and went without him suspecting a thing. Perhaps this meant that there was something about him, something he was completely unaware of, that irreversibly fused her to him in the same way her air of completeness tethered him to her, and that was why she had kept it a secret until now and never really left him at all.

When he reflected most deeply about their relationship, most recently while drinking Jack Daniels and staring out the square-framed window into the garden of their rented house in Pozega, he guessed it was his drive for worldly success - something she lacked in spite of her passion for music - that fascinated her and ultimately kept them together. Sure he was restless and always felt inadequate, but wasn't that the main reason he was successful? It was always *difference* that brought people together, he proudly concluded as he filled his glass with the last drops of bourbon. In nature there were symbiotic relationships everywhere. So why not in love? But perhaps he was just drunk and it was just her opportunism that kept her with him after the affair. The diplomat broke it off when she got too serious and when it was clear that she had to get out of Croatia Anderson was her safest bet. She had already deceived him once, therefore breaking the trust and sanctity that existed between them, and was only hanging on until they could land on their feet in some safer situation where she could bide her time before hooking up with the first decent guy that came her way.

II

Anderson woke up at four in the morning to the beeping of his wristwatch. He quickly dressed without awaking Anna and then rolled up their sleeping bags and stuffed their backpacks with enough food to last them the six days he guessed it would take to get to the border. Since their house was furnished by the owner the only items they stood to lose were excess clothing and whatever personal possessions they had accumulated over the course of their stay in Croatia. He woke up Anna at seven, brusquely pulling the curtains open as he leaned over the bed. She dressed quickly and quietly and ten minutes later they were well on their way, already passing beneath the tall Gothic arch that marked the entrance to the center of the village as they followed the main road past a small brick mill and then an abandoned kiln. Half an hour later the village was already fading from sight, the large baroque fountain in the center of the park now just a gray blur in the middle of an ocean of green.

Anderson took Anna's hand and guided her along a narrow dirt path on the edge of the forest. The path was lined with rose bushes and tall slender trees, tiny green bulbs hanging from their white spidery boughs.

"Where are we going to sleep tonight?" she asked, rubbing the knuckles of her thumbs in her eyes as she yawned. The path opened up into a small clearing that gave the impression it may once have been a secret meeting place, so perfectly was it enclosed on all sides by a continuous wall of tall serried pines. The natural arena was disrupted at two other points by what looked like entrances to narrow pathways similar to the one they had just traversed.

"We can make it in five days," he replied. The incongruity of this answer to her question struck him in mid speech. For a moment the strange thought occurred to him that she might take it as an attempt to disguise the fact that he was not really taking her to Hungary, but rather on some sort of treacherous journey that could only end in disaster, something he had secretly concocted as a punishment for her infidelity. "We'll start looking for some kind of natural shelter later in the day," he said to reassure her.

When their eyes met again she had an expression on her face that he had never seen before. It was one that spoke of something different than reconciliation and love.

"You know, I've put up with you for a long time," she said objectively. The tone of her voice was like that of an advocate addressing a magistrate, without a trace of malice or emotion. "When we lived in New York you were always complaining that the world wasn't right for you as though you should have been born into a different existence, one with a completely different set of talents and friends. Then you convinced me we should move to Yugoslavia out of some mock humanitarian cause that was really just your own desire to escape from the prison you had built around yourself over all those years of wishing you were something other than what you actually were. And no doubt you secretly wished that I was different as well. I should hate you." She paused and looked at him in a theatrical way as though she had just made her final case to some invisible jury. "And I do," she stated solemnly. "With all my heart I hate you. You say I am the thing that keeps you most from being what you are meant to become. Why else would I have had an affair with that vulgar Frenchman if you hadn't driven me to it?"

She tilted her head back and took a long slow breath and as though guided by the same impulse, her eyes softened and she looked suddenly gentler. They walked side by side to the center of the clearing, making careful and deliberate steps to avoid slipping on the surface of the long wet grass. He wished it were night so they could stare blankly into the vast starry firmament and forget about all the anguish they had brought each other.

But however much he would have liked to deny it, the majority of her accusations were true. In all his years in New York he felt that his life was governed by an external cause that he had no control over, one that created unwanted traction in his life that he was always forced to react against. Did he marry Anna because he loved her or because he wanted to escape his fears of one day becoming nothing? Did he become a journalist because his father told him when he was young that only men with exciting careers were attractive to women or because he really loved writing and travelling? Since his father had never been an outgoing or reasonable man, rarely socializing with others and spending most of his time alone in his study, it would have been easy for Anderson to discredit anything he said. Yet for some reason these words had influenced Anderson all the way through school and university, becoming a banner for the same power that always pervaded his adult life and force him to *react against* rather than *forge his way through* the world according to his own inner directive.

Although these feelings were never strong enough to push him to the brink of crisis, he was aware of them in the same way a man may be aware of a faint scent in the air without having to focus all of his attention on it. Sometimes these emotions were brought forth in a series of dreams in which he was the author of a poorly received novel he had intended as an avant garde literary experiment. Instead of wowing the cutting edge New York literary critics, the novel fell flat on its face and ended up selling for half price in the cult literature section of an East Village record store next to rows of garish books on American pop culture, including one with nude photo spreads of secret motorcycle gangs who covered their bodies head-to-toe in green and red paint in order to express their devotion to some apocryphal Mexican god. In these dreams he read the book over and over again desperately thinking of a way he could revise and republish it, claiming to the readers and reviewers that the original version had just been transcribed incorrectly by the publishers, yet the dream would always end with a confrontation with an editor in a New York restaurant where all the customers seemed to know exactly what they were talking about and by the looks on their faces clearly sided with the editor. Then his unconsciously mind would exit the dream and become only partially aware of the room around him. In his state of half-wakefulness the book became a metaphor for his failed attempts at living the life he wanted rather than the one he had and that he – Anderson as himself - in his dream was also somehow aware of this. As he listened to the random creaking of the house and the hypnotic vibrations of the refrigerator he sometimes toyed with the thought that the character he was in his dream experienced concrete reality as an expression of his subconscious in much the same way that Jung postulated our dreams were an expression of our unconscious. Thus what was normally held as reality for us, was really just a dream world for those entities that peopled our dreams. As the first rays of dawn broke over the horizon, he would always fall back into a deep and empty sleep out of which he would emerge in the morning with no recollection of the dream nor his troubled sleep the night before. He would only remember the dream at random moments in his life while sitting in a café or walking down the street, and so he never knew exactly *when* he had dreamed this, but only that he *had* lived through that troubling sequence of events that could only have been a dream.

Anna loosened the collar of her sweater and looked up at the sky. Two small clouds met at a point in the sky directly above the place they were standing and then took on a new and unrecognizable shape. A bird of prey described a wide ark beneath the clouds and then vanished from sight.

"These are times of great upheaval," she said clearly in a half whisper. Her tone was oratorical. "But I'm sure we can make it. I've always been more optimistic than you. That's why we have survived so long. But, do you know how I know we will pull through?" Anderson shrugged his shoulders. "There's something about the way the sun is filtering through the leaves that reminds me of *Tallis*." It was her pet name for a work by Vaughn Williams she had always associated with beauty and redemption at the long end of suffering. "The violins especially."

"What do you mean by that?" he asked, although he really knew what she meant. She always took random objects and events in life as signposts of hope or impending tragedy. Her world was one of hidden meanings and emotional nuances, while his was one of success or failure, devoid of anything outside these two disparate and empty poles.

She didn't respond, instead grabbing his forearm and pulling him towards one of the paths on the other side of the clearing in much the same way that a little girl might grab the hand of an uncle or older house visitor to guide him away to show off her doll collection. Yet there was also something solemn about it, as though the gesture was hiding some grave feeling that she had alluded to in her last comment, but he had somehow failed to detect. He felt weak, almost ridiculous. It was likely she had more dirt to reveal to him concerning the affair and was just waiting for the ideal moment to tell him, perhaps when they were surrounded by a horde of Serbian troops and he had no other choice but to defend her.

She let his hand drop as if to signal she had detected his sudden change of mood. They crossed the threshold of a second forest and worked their way down a narrow brambled path, which seemed to ascend and descend in random increments, turning right and left without any sense of higher order. Later they walked over a small wooden footbridge spanning a shallow, rocky brook that made a gurgling sound they had heard from deeper in the forest, only greatly magnified, giving the impression they had been approaching a great river rather than a small trickling stream.

The air filled with a scent like wet flowers as they followed a narrow path up the side of a small mountain to an area where there were several large boulders strewn about like marbles arranged by a race of giants. The sun was beginning to set and the boulders would provide the best cover possible to unfold their sleeping bags for the night. Anderson looked at Anna and for a moment; even though darkness was coming, the world lit up like a beam of light shining through a pane of leaded glass. Everything she had ever been to him seemed suddenly different and he knew that from this moment onward nothing could ever be taken for granted.

III

The next morning they reached the end of the forest – dense and dark with its towering blue fir trees and tall thick nettles – and then they crossed a river, following the northern bank until they reached a small lake that was not on any map Anderson had seen. Anna wiped the water off her legs and rolled down her pants. The sun was at its zenith and a flock of birds flew overhead in a broken V-shaped pattern. The clear tranquil waters of the lake glittered before them, the surface still and without ripples even in the gentle breeze as though it were not water they were looking at but some other substance like glass or liquid metal. Anderson stopped and turned around, taking a quick look at the landscape around him. Although he had never been here before everything seemed strangely familiar as though witnessed before on some terrestrial blueprint now locked away in his ancestral memory.

"Are we near Velika yet?" she asked.

"Yes," he said. "But we have to avoid it completely and stay off the main roads."

He walked over to a charred tree and knelt down beside it. Somewhere outside of Velika there was said by local legend to be a makeshift monument marked by a burned tree, its broken branch apparently hanging out over the opening of a small lake nested in a mountain basin located on the other side of the forest from which they had just emerged. Stories Anderson had heard in countless variations had several features in common: a Croatian soldier had stopped there to drink out of the lake and was ambushed by a small battalion of seven Serbian infantry. When the Croatian surrendered, instead of taking him prisoner, the Serbians forced the man at gun point to hang himself, threatening to cut him into tiny pieces bit by bit if he didn't comply with their demand. Since that day every one of the original seven Serbians had died in combat. A superstitious old woman who sold magazines at a kiosk in Pozega claimed that when the wind howled at night near that lake it was really the Croat's ghost laughing at the Serbians, whose souls had all ended up in some bleaker form of afterlife or damnation.

"This place was once just a place," Anna said in a whisper. A small bird flew overhead and landed on the branch of the charred tree in front of them. The surface of the icy lake glistened and rippled in a sudden sharp wind from the mountain like an infinite sheet of chain mail. "A nothing of a place that was here as if only by accident, but still caries traces of its nothingness just by virtue of its being here."

She began to hum a tune that Anderson immediately recognized from the first time he had taken her home. They were in a small café in Geneva and in her left hand she was carrying a book she had just bought. She was wearing a pullover with blue and white horizontal stripes that made her look much younger – like a teenage girl from a rave. The song was playing somewhere out on the street, in a car, or on a portable stereo, or sitting unseen on the sidewalk outside.

"I can still picture the way you looked that first night," he said, wondering if she would pick up on what he was talking about.

"You remembered the tune?" She seemed surprised. "That was when I was smoking a lot of dope," she said. "And I bet you still don't know what it is."

"Hum it again," he said.

"That's not the point. You were always in your own world of little successes. And you still are. When I just made the comment about the tree you were listening to my whistling thinking about a time when we first went out. And that night we first went out you were probably thinking of some other girl friend or maybe what it would be like if you ever got me alone beside an icy mountain lake."

"And here we are..." he said slowly, contemplatively. "Everything is so beautiful." Inside he felt differently. Her words almost hurt him. They seemed like the kind of things that someone who detested him might say, not a person he loved or even once loved.

"I know you too well," she said. "Or maybe because of this I don't know you at all." Her face was tight and drawn in a way he had never seen before. It was as though her lifelong disguise had been torn away to reveal a second person, one that bore no relation to the woman he once married. "We could cross this lake a thousand times and each time you would be a different you, but never once would you really be you. The world dissolves away from us. It's like that text you have inside of you always changing and always becoming something other than it is, yet at the same time always showing you up for the fake you are and the things you aren't. But I loved you anyway and loved you with all my soul as though there weren't another being in the entire universe. And without a trace of regret."

"And what do you have to contribute to the world?" he asked. "You go through life as if somehow the world couldn't make do without you and your reflections."

"Nothing," she said. Then she broke out laughing like a person who thought of something so private and obscure its humor could never be related to anyone. "This place and all its mythology...is nothing. Nothing at all." She paused and shrugged her shoulders. "So what lies further on? What is ultimately more isolated, nothing, or those things that are on the fringes of nothing, as though one step further removed from the core of emptiness?"

"But to fall away from nothing is to gain foothold in the world and begin to become something."

A dark blue bird with a twisted beak and a tall flat crest landed on a branch above them and started grooming its wing. In the distance they could hear a deep rumbling as though an avalanche had just hit an unseen mountain slope.

As they made their way around the perimeter of the lake a silence fell between them. For the longest time the forest almost seemed to vanish and he imagined he was standing in front of her when she first confessed to her affair. He was reading the entertainment section of a local English newspaper and she was in the kitchen making her usual cup of Darjeeling tea.

"I've been sleeping with someone else," she said. The words came out quickly and painlessly in a way that suggested she had had enough of holding it in and was just trying to get it over with regardless of the consequences. There was a loud metallic clang and she stepped out of the kitchen. She walked over and sat down beside him, pulling the newspaper away from him as she folded it in half. She set it on the floor beside his feet. His first thought was that she wasn't serious and was just playing a game with him to see how he would react. Not that it seemed absurd that any other man would want her, as she was perhaps even more beautiful – steeped with the wisdom of age that an older face can draw into its radiance – than when he had first met her. In Geneva there was the odd occasional comment, a sudden flash of greed or churlishness that was more than just a glimpse of the last remnants of a moody and unfinished person that had all but ceased to exist since she left home to go to university. Standing beside a Romanesque church that had been converted into a post office and later a discotheque she had once even hollered at him for buying her the wrong kind of sparkling water. But all that was gone and all that remained was the beauty of a woman in her prime. No. It would not have been – and obviously wasn't – such an impossibility for her to sleep with someone else. It had just never occurred to him that she might be unfaithful as he had begun to view the world as a composite entity involving Anna at every level of his experience. If in the future he would ever do something, it would be with her. Even if he went away, as he often did for several days on business or just a long solitary walk around the outskirts of Pozega, he would always be going away *from* her, and hence she was even a part of his solitude.

When she finally turned her head back to look into his eyes he could tell by the deep furrow in her brow that it wasn't a joke and he felt suddenly out of place, like a clown at a funeral or something equally grave and serious.

"Why?" he asked softly. The light in the room had dimmed and Anderson sensed the entire world had suddenly gone dark. Out of the corner of his eye he watched a shadow moving across the wall. It was flat and large and distorted out of all proportions as though cast by some kind of hideous animal or mythological beast that was scurrying across the floor behind him. He blinked and the shadow was gone.

"I don't know," she said. "But it's over. That much I know."

"So does that mean everything will go back to normal?" he asked in a way he hoped would come off sounding more naïve than sarcastic.

"Nothing is ever normal," she said. Then she went to the other side of the room and started a deep breathing exercise as though he wasn't even in the room. He walked outside and didn't return until she was in bed.

She had apparently started seeing the French diplomat – Hugo was his name, six months after they had moved to what was then Yugoslavia. "Everything is so primal here," she said to Anderson that night of her confession as she pulled the covers over to her side and swept her hair back. "You can see it in the black eyes of the villagers. You can feel it in the dark midnight air. You can see it in the mountain peaks. They look like they're covered with a strange kind of magical lint that reminds me of an evil forest in some kind of fairy tail." Anderson was unconvinced but looked at her with a tenderness and pathos that he couldn't control. "I never found Hugo attractive," she went on to tell him in a hushed and almost secretive tone. "He was not special and I never loved him. It could have been anybody," she said. Anderson wondered if that meant it could also have been him if he had not in fact been married to her at the time. "I was overcome with an uncontrollable desire to make love to him for no other reason but to have sex in its purest and most insubstantial form. I wanted to tear away all my shackles and become like those maddening horns and cymbals at the crescendo in *A Rite of Spring*." She coughed and then got up to get a glass of water. "We all need to become *somebody* sometime," she shouted from the bathroom. Then he heard the sound of her gargling. When she came back she crawled into bed and turned away from him as if to signal the end of her confession.

Night had already fallen and all they had was time. Anderson knew he could find out more if he wanted to. But he didn't. What she had revealed was already enough to anger him and enough to make sure he didn't want to hear any more. She hadn't *really* left him. She was still his. Yet for the first time since he first kissed her, anything was possible. Anything. He could be a fool and let her get away with it while secretly hating her. He could be strong and truly forgive her. Or he could wait and have his own affair – but at some later date when she was convinced that he truly loved her and would never love another. Yet was that really him? As he watched her crumpled form move up and down to the rhythm of her breathing, the only thing he was truly sure of was that he didn't know what he really felt and what he really wanted to do. All of his options seemed to trickle down from some higher source that was ultimately exterior to him. Get back at her out of service to those who had once said he was too soft. Forgive her because people always said one should forgive and forget and for no other reason. He couldn't deny that he still loved her, but he was also the last person on Earth to say she hadn't behaved like a lying slut in sleeping on a regular basis with a man with whom she only wanted to experience sex in its purest form. But if this motive of hers was really true, why did she have to sleep with Hugo more than once? Habitual sexual encounters always had a sense of regiment and ritual about them and for this reason could hardly be described as carnal. But maybe this meant she did love Hugo after all and craved to see him over and over again, even though she was too proud to admit it. Or maybe, he thought as his mind began to wander off into the web of disjoint hypnotic noises the night could always spin, Hugo was just a lousy screw – he imagined a cartoon Frenchman wearing a beret, his pants half off holding a cigar in his hand while he huffed and puffed through his mustache in a vain effort to get an erection - and she had to try over and over again to get what she ultimately learned she would never get from the man. If this was true, then she might cheat on him again for the same reason. As he listened to the incessant dripping of a distant faucet, he came to the conclusion that something irrational and maybe even evil – although he was loath to use this word as it had a sense of melodrama about it that he found distasteful - had just happened and that it might happen again and that he wasn't sure how he felt about it or what he should do, but knew with the deepest conviction that it might happen again.

By the time they reached the far side of the lake it was almost dark. In the fading light, the surroundings conjured forth a sense of pervasive hollowness at the center of which he and Anna were hovering. He felt for a moment that he didn't exist beyond the small set of perceptions built up from the scenery around him and his memories, now almost entirely clouded by Anna and her recent exploits. Before they had reached the charred tree, with the danger of their escape still dominating their thoughts, the affair had conveniently slipped into the background. But now it was back. And whatever he was going to do about it, between now and the time they got to the Hungarian border and even further on into the future when they returned to America, not even he knew.

They followed the icy line of the lake until they reached a gravel pit that looked like it had once been a small mine. The pit was roped off and at the base was an old rusted service vehicle that had been turned on its roof. The windows had been smashed and the seats inside were torn and blackened. The pit was about fifty yards in diameter, sloping gently downwards from a narrow wooded strip that formed a natural wall, hemming in the waters of the lake. He wondered if these waters ever overflowed past the wooded strip and into the pit during seasons of high tide and, if they didn't, why not. Perhaps whoever had dug the pit knew the habits and patterns of the lake well enough not to make a some fatal mistake that could ultimately lead to a disaster in which dozens of miners drowned.

"Don't you think we should stop here?" Anna asked in the tone of a strong suggestion.

"To sleep?" Anderson turned to her and raised his eyebrows.

"I'm tired and it's getting dark." She lifted up her arm and pointed over to a small patch of trees that formed a natural shelter at the base of the mountain to the left of the gravel pit. "This looks like a good place."

Anderson nodded his head and they walked towards the line of trees. The air had a fresh minty scent that reminded him of two things: a summer he had once spent in upstate New York when he was ten and was still young enough to have an older cousin take him horseback riding, and the smell of a pistol after it has just been shot. Why it reminded him of the summer was obvious: the scent of the countryside. But why it reminded him of a freshly fired gun, he wasn't sure. It was one of those things like why you liked one girl and not another or dreamed one night of someone you knew but never really thought about. It was in that region of experience one had no control over and never would. Psychologists spent years trying to make up reasons why people made certain connections, but the bottom line was that nobody knew. Anything could happen and it wasn't fair to ask why. There were few concrete laws and even fewer explanations to back them up.

When they reached the small wooded area they unpacked their sleeping bags and set them ceremoniously on the ground one beside the other, almost as though they had unconsciously agreed to make it resemble as much as possible a bedroom in which a married couple might sleep. Anderson threw his coat at the foot of his sleeping bag and stretched out his arms.

"I always loathed camping," she said. He didn't reply. It was one of those unproductive comments people blurted out automatically without any real conviction when they were too tired to think of anything interesting to say. He felt strangely relieved that she was in a bad mood, because that meant she wouldn't expect him to act like he was in a better mood than he really was.

"So did I," he finally replied.

When it was almost dark and Anna was almost asleep and the only light was that coming off the lake from an unseen moon he imagined was rising behind the Papuk Mountain he knew was close but couldn't see. He heard a soft and low-pitched noise that gradually gained in substance and definition until he identified a man's voice. Just when he was about to shake Anna's arm, the voice disappeared into the vapory silence of the night. Anderson stopped and listened. He heard nothing but the sound of the wind blowing across the lake.

For almost twenty minutes he lay there beside her listening until he was sure the noise had gone or that it had been a figment of his imagination all along. At one point he turned and looked over at Anna and pulled out a small twig from under her head. Her eyes were closed but he could sense in her a kind of tranquillity that almost made him forget that they were alone in the forest, and ultimately the world, and that whatever happened between them for as long as they lived, no matter how important it seemed, would only matter to them and no one else. It was a feeling both good and bad, like nothing he had ever experienced before, leaving behind it a sense of lacking and despair that somehow seemed magnified to infinite proportions in the darkness of the night, thoughts of the mountain looming somewhere in the distance cross-woven with those memories of the voice he heard or just thought he heard. He let his neck relax and slowly fell asleep, all the time wishing he could wake up Anna and tell her everything he was thinking.

IV

Anderson awoke to the sound of a man coughing from somewhere no further than the nearest trees, although he could not see anybody. The air hung still without any breeze and the sky was flooded with a faint silver light that seemed to stretch no further than the periphery of his vision, giving the impression that the world was about to be engulfed by a vast ocean of darkness. Anderson leaned over towards Anna, but before he had a chance to shake her arm he saw the dim outline of a man towering over him. The light of the moon was just strong enough to illuminate the coils of smoke twisting around his troubled youthful face. Anderson stared into the man's eyes. There was something sullen, yet shriven or absolved about his expression, as though he had been sent on a strange unearthly mission to purge the world of its iniquities. The man was wearing dark colored fatigues and had small burrs stuck to his legs. His lightly scarred face gleamed in the smoke and light as he stood there silently, apparently waiting for Anderson to say something, but he didn't.

"Hello," the man finally said with caution, his eyes surreptitiously searching beyond Anderson's figure out into the line of trees behind him. He had an accent that Anderson thought was Croatian, although he could not be sure. The man pulled a flashlight out of his coat pocket and shined it on the ground.

Anderson pursed his lips and let his gaze drop out of focus. He was not fully awake before the words of the German philosopher Martin Heidegger began to wend their way through his mind: *But the song still remains, which names the land over which it sings. What is the song itself? How is a mortal capable of it? Whence does it sing? How far does it reach into the abyss?* He had not thought of this passage since completing his fourth year project thesis. As the soldier stood there before him they seemed suddenly relevant, however in a way that was neither obvious nor even remotely tangible. Life - or all those things that he had come to realize were entirely unknowable yet still forced him to think, feel, and act - was happening that very moment and he had no control over its outcome.

"Hello," Anderson finally replied. Anna stirred beside him.

Anderson took a deep breath and stood up. Anna opened her eyes. She had a crisp and alert expression that made him wonder if she had been secretly awake for hours listening to the sound of his every breath.

"What's going on?" she said. "Who is this?"

"I mean no harm," the soldier said as Anna lifted herself out of her sleeping bag. He turned around and looked at her and then turned back to Anderson. "I'm alone. I disserted from the army. I couldn't take it any more. I'd rather get killed myself than kill another."

"We're crossing into Hungary," Anderson said. He was now sure the man was a Croat. "The Serbian Army was advancing on our village." But after the words left his mouth he felt he had already revealed too much.

Anna stepped past the soldier and took Anderson by the wrist. She held it for a moment as though to take his pulse. Then she let it drop.

"And the woman?" the soldier asked. He looked at Anna and tilted his head in what seemed like momentary recognition. Perhaps, Anderson thought, she resembled an old lover; maybe even the man's first.

"I'm going with him."

"The pass is dangerous," the soldier said with slow admonishment. "There are bands of rebels just over the mountain. And rumors of a massacre near the border to Serbian territory."

"Where are you going?" Anna asked.

"Hungary. Just like you." His tone almost seemed surly.

"Than maybe you can join us," Anna said in an overly earnest way that bothered Anderson.

"You look like NATO officers. How do I know you won't send me back to my country when we get there?"

"My husband is a journalist. We're just trying to get out of here."

The soldier set his backpack down recklessly, without waiting for a response. "Believe me. You'd be foolish to cross unarmed." He looked up to the sky. "Five thousand dollars. For safety. I'll take you to the Barcs and you pay me five thousand."

"We don't have that kind of money," Anna said. "How about we just help each other for free?"

The soldier nodded his head and smiled, the threat of his unexpected presence seeming to dissipate. "I will sleep over there," he said, pointing to a space in the trees about twenty yards away. Then he picked up his backpack and vanished into the forest, the sound of his feet crunching through the gravel filling the air behind him. Anderson crawled back into his sleeping bag and kissed Anna lightly on her neck before closing his eyes, although he was not able to fall asleep.

The night passed slowly. Occasionally Anderson heard the soldier cough and mutter something in a language Anderson didn't recognize. In his deepest phase of sleep, Anderson lost all awareness of the world around him. Anna and the soldier vanished from his mind and he imagined he was in the middle of a clear and shallow lake where a number of boats had gathered by the shore. He heard screams and hollers of joy as the inhabitants of the boats hauled in enormous fish the size of a man's leg. From a distance they looked like they were wrapped in gold foil, so much did they shine in the Sun. Anderson looked down at the water – in which he was now floating at chin level – and saw a large shimmering form move from underneath his feet. When he ducked in the water to grab for it, the fish disappeared. Despondent over his failure to catch what could have been the largest fish of the day, he swam to the shore to see if he might join the other fishermen and share in their luck. But when he got there the boats were gone and the sky had darkened. He crawled up onto the dock and looked down into the now muddy waters. He saw what looked like hundreds of smaller fish of a similar type moving gracefully through the water. He lay down chest first on the dock and tried to catch them with his hands, yet every time he tried to grab one, it slipped through his fingers, almost seeming to melt into the water like a sliver of ice.

In the morning small tufts fog scattered like pieces of torn cloth across the landscape slowly emerged from the darkness and then vanished again like images gradually appearing on photographic paper only to become blanched and eventually vanish into whiteness when left in developing fluid to long. After what seemed like hours, he heard a loud noise like a stone falling at the end of a long metal sewer pipe and then opened his eyes to find Anna shaking his shoulder.

"It's getting late," she said.

Anderson stretched his arms and back and looked out towards the lake where a flock of herons had gathered, dragging their legs silently through the water. The wind blew strongly, making a series of rolling creases on the surface of the lake.

"What time is it?" he asked. Although he had always been punctual, he had never owned a watch, preferring instead to guess the time, taking satisfaction that he was usually right within five or ten minutes. It was a talent he secretly linked to his being connected to some great universal clock that ticked outside of earthly time, yet always marked its passage. But since moving to Yugoslavia he felt detached from this figurative timepiece and therefore somewhat numbed to the sensation, abstract or real, of the passing of time.

"I'm not sure," she said. "But Janos is getting impatient."

"Who?" The name was unfamiliar. For a moment he thought she was referring to some small animal – perhaps a rabbit - she might have captured and befriended while he was sleeping.

She looked at him strangely and arched her eyebrow. "Last night," she said.

He scratched his head. Then it came back to him, the image of the soldier looming over him from the night before. "Where is he?"

"He went to wash in the lake."

They set off when the sun had almost reached its zenith. After scaling to the top of a long slope marking the beginning of the Papuk Mountains they passed through a sub-alpine meadow thriving with small purple clovers and tall yellow weeds. On either side a flat gray mass of rock rose upward to meet the sky. These were the *heartlands*, Anderson thought without really knowing what he meant. There was something about the smell of clovers in the air, the glitter of sunlight on the deep green blades of grass that made him feel he was in the presence of some life-giving force which, if he nurtured properly, would bring him greater health and prosperity than he had ever known before. While he was initially suspicious of the soldier, the meadow, or *heartlands* as it were, naturally conjured forth feelings of trust and communion. Certainly, Anderson thought as they approached the edge of a forested area marked by almost mathematical rows of equidistant birch trees standing about fifteen feet apart, having a third person present was a good thing, as it diluted the tension between him and Anna and focussed their thoughts on the common goal of crossing the mountains and making it to the border.

Almost an hour after they had passed into this new forest – a period during which not a word was spoken – they stopped abruptly and all at once by a small river as though paying heed to an invisible cue. There were blue-green leaves hanging delicately from tall white-barked trees and the ground was soft and matted with moss and splinters of decaying wood. As they rested by the riverbank, Anderson noticed that Anna was paying more attention to the soldier than she had at first, more than he felt comfortable with. Since entering the forest their interactions had been ones of occasional smiles or sighs. It seemed their ability to speak had been truncated and that their only form of communication was one of ambiguous physical gestures where moments of utter silence functioned as periods or gaps between parts of a greater text. But this was clearly a break in this pattern. Anna watched his nostrils and lips with careful attention as though trying to read like sheet music the subtle inflections of the young man's face. However the soldier, seeming to have received an unspoken nomination as leader, appeared oblivious to Anna's attention, instead looking directly ahead like a man dedicated to performing his job as carefully as possible without revealing the slightest hint that he had any doubt about his qualifications for the position.

Before setting off from the riverbank the soldier leaned over and started carving in the ground with a stick what looked like the outline of a house. Anderson burst out laughing when the image of the young man working on a conveyor belt in a Stalinist factory entered his mind. Indeed, he was leading them through the mountains with the same mechanical disposition that such a man in a factory might possess. The soldier turned around and gave Anderson a sharp look as though he had just done something to break the unspoken pact of silence between them, although it seemed to Anderson that the soldier's silence was a kind of *rupturing* in its own right. Silence, *yes*, he thought. But your kind of silence?

"Laughter has its place," Anna said in a calm but punctuated way as though she knew what Anderson was thinking. But the look on her face also suggested she had formed a secret allegiance to the soldier and was scolding Anderson for calling out the young man's authority.

"And I'm sure you know it well," Anderson retorted.

The soldier burst out laughing, but in a way that wasn't spontaneous and rich, inviting Anderson and Anna to participate and share in its resonance, but subtlety mocking, not of any one thing in particular, but of all things in general.

Anna raised her eyebrow and looked at the soldier.

"So, you're a journalist?" the soldier asked Anderson.

"And you're a soldier," Anderson said.

"And I am nothing," said Anna.

"Perhaps it is best to be nothing," the soldier said. Then he put his arm around Anna in a playful but still arrogant way and kissed her head, all the while looking directly at Anderson. "That way nobody will have anything against you." Anna pulled away, but in a slow and languorous way that made Anderson uncomfortable.

The three started walking along the riverbank and soon found a place to cross. It was late afternoon and Anderson was already feeling tired. In his working life back in New York, when he shared an office with other writers and publishers, he had always feared the dull lagging hours of the afternoon with nothing to carry him through but the promise of the coming night when the city lights would start to glow and he would feel alive and possessed by their cool white magnificence. It wasn't that he disliked the world of publishers and career men – he actually loved working with other people and couldn't imagine being apart from them; this was the reason he had become a journalist instead of something more solitary and intellectual. Did he have a fear of being alone? If so, how could he ever be a novelist if this entailed sitting alone all those long hours leaning over a typewriter isolated from the very people he was writing about? Perhaps this was another reason he had fallen in love with Anna. She was a creative artist in so far as she was a concert quality violinist, but at the same time she was also brimming over with life and social spontaneity, a gregarious flirt and lover of all people.

Half an hour later they passed over a small hill, the side of which seemed to have fallen away in some kind of avalanche centuries before leaving a vertical wall of striped rock in its wake. Anderson turned to Anna, relishing for a moment the memory of the gentle yet enigmatic creature he had fallen in love with years before. The soft rouge of her cheeks matched the color of a patch of star-shaped flowers covering a hill to their left. How perfect she looked. So perfect, in fact, he almost felt inadequate standing beside her. Even though she had cheated on him, even though she seemed to enjoy the soldier's bold advance – although he admitted to himself that it may not have been an advance at all and he had just perceived it as such from the vantage point of his own insecurities – she was still perfect. She had somehow woven her imperfections into a greater canvass of absolute perfection. With Anna he had sometimes felt he was making mistakes even when things were going well. This was a sign that he truly loved her. As he accelerated his pace to keep up with the soldier he wondered if other people felt the same way and if this was, in fact, a lack of strength that she could detect in him. Would her life be better with someone else, someone more rugged and insensitive, a person completely impervious to her beauty?

When the air had cooled down – signaling the coming of evening – they came upon a natural stone terrace the size of a football field. The ground was covered with shale and, in a few places, clovers and tall green weeds grew up through the fissures in the rock. Tall majestic trees surrounded them on all sides, giving the impression that they were standing in the middle of a great auditorium awaiting the arrival of some secret procession. The soldier took a deep breath and turned to Anderson.

"What do you have for food?" he asked.

Anderson looked over at Anna, who had packed what few remnants she could find before they abandoned their house in the village.

"Not much," she said. "I brought some bread and cheese. We were counting on no more than six days and didn't want to weigh ourselves down."

"I have a can of fish," the soldier said. "If someone has a can opener?"

"Here?" Anna broke out in deep gargling laughter. "I think we need a blender as well!"

"So," said the soldier. "I have to use a rock?"

"I guess so," she said whimsically. She laughed again under her breath.

Anderson walked over to a pile of rocks that occupied the center of the terrace, the strange arrangement apparently left behind by a receding glacier thousands of years before and never touched by human hands. He bent down and picked up a piece of slate, which, with its flat curved forms spreading out in three directions, looked like some kind of Asian dagger used only for obscure religious rituals and ceremonial killings. He threw it at the ground and watched it shatter into dozens of small pieces. Then he picked up one of the shards and walked back to show Anna and the soldier, who were now hunched down beside one another like two children inside a cramped and invisible fort.

"Am I interrupting something?" Anderson asked. Anna shifted away from the soldier. "Janos was just telling me about his family," she said in the self-righteous tone of a person who has just been cleared of a false accusation. "He says that he has three sisters and a dog."

Anderson smiled to diffuse the tension and handed the soldier the sharp piece of stone. The solider accepted it without a word and began to pry open the can of fish with it.

"I hope you like lamprey," he said. "In Latvia it is a delicacy. You can even get it in a bar, just like your American French fries and chicken wings." He said the word "your" in a pointed and accusing manner as though Anderson was singly responsible for everything bad about America. It was an attitude he had encountered often in Yugoslavia.

Anna smiled at the two men peacefully, the way she used to when she had just finished practicing. She looked at the can and broke out laughing. "Lamprey? I love it," she said with sarcastic enthusiasm. "I spent a whole year eating the stuff in college. You could say I was a real *sucker* for lamprey."

The solider smiled in apparent acknowledgement of her humor, and handed the open can to her. She pulled out a dark slender form and dropped it into her mouth. She closed her jaws and then froze for a moment before spitting it out on the ground in front of her. "I'm sorry. I just can't..."

"Now you try," the soldier said, looking directly at Anderson. He took out a Lamprey and handed it to Anderson, who proceeded to swallow the sleek black form whole without the slightest flinch or contortion in his face. "And you," the soldier said to Anna, "You should eat some of the bread you brought."

They finished eating and continued across the mountain. As the sun set the sky turned from blue to pink and gold and then finally to a rich violet that mirrored the tiny violet crowns of the thousands of clovers and also mirrored the tinted hues of the massive stone forms around them that now seemed more violet than gray in the strange unearthly light. A crow flew overhead and landed on an oblong boulder as though it were waiting for them to come over and greet it. A warm wind suddenly blew from the north and the crow flew away like an emissary obeying its summons. By this time it was almost dark and the sky had assumed a deep inky hue. They quickly collected whatever kindling they could find at the edge of the woods and built a small fire beside the pile of rocks.

Anderson sat down across from and beside Anna and the soldier, completing a neat triangle around the fire they had just built. He watched the tongues of orange and yellow flame lapping forth from the center of the hearth. For a lingering moment he was overcome by a feeling that whatever happened in life between people and to people was always in the end good and that it was only through interactions with new acquaintances that one could open oneself up to his feelings while also renewing their relationships with loved ones. In such a way the soldier's presence had made him see Anna in a new and more beautiful light. He watched her staring into the orange fingers of fire crackling and sparking upwards into the blackness of the night. This was the *inner text* he had imagined but never before touched, the inspiration behind his recurring dream about the widely ridiculed experimental novel he had written, although this was the way the novel should have been. *Life as a master text.* The world as the perfect set of words and impressions weaving in and out of our lives and the lives of those around us.

With this immensely satisfying feeling tucked neatly away inside him, Anderson withdrew early, preferring to lie alone in his sleeping bag to stare at the stars while listening to the soft sound of his wife's voice as she spoke beside the fire with the soldier. In his mind he summoned up strange and exotic landscapes and even played a mental game, the goal of which was to discover hidden symmetries and parallels in these imagined worlds. There were six steeples of equal height but only four masks (all different) and not a single sword or lance to be seen anywhere. A point on the far horizon made a triangle with the peak of the dark-capped mountain and the snout of the leopard basking nearest to the castle, but the same point made a rhombus with the helmets of the three riders crossing the small footbridge in front of the castle.

Just as he was about to fall asleep, his sense of harmony was broken by the sound of thunder in the distance. He sat awake for the next five minutes, a time over which he must have shifted his body at least seven or eight times to get into the most comfortable position. When he was just about ready to close his eyes and descend back into his relaxing world of hidden patterns and secret geometries, Anna laughed in a girlish and vulnerable way that he hadn't heard since the first year they were together. Although he was too far away to hear exactly what was being said, there was a familiar note of tenderness and yielding in her laughter that was too strong to ignore. It was a laughter only shown to him in her most intimate moments. It was the laughter of a woman opening up to someone, experiencing feelings of closeness and trust. His geometric world vanished and he felt suddenly angry inside. Ho naïve he was to think that the Frenchman had not also heard her laugh that way, and that under some tree or bridge she had not stared into his eyes and laughed the very same way she had always laughed to Anderson that first year they were together?

There was a sudden hush and he was seized by the impulse that he should get up and walk over to the hearth to defend his marriage. What right did this Croatian paramour have to butt into his life at a time when he and his wife were trying to heal their relationship while also fleeing from a dangerous attack on their village? He imagined himself charging at the soldier, shirtsleeves rolled up as he brandished a burning stick in the young man's face. That would certainly change his tune, he thought, emphasizing the word "tune" in his mind in a way that he knew Anna would have taken as an attempt to insult her for never becoming a top-flight concert violinist if she were able to somehow climb inside his head and monitor his thoughts. All the better, anyway. And what was she doing opening up to the soldier in such a suggestive way? Maybe he was wrong to accuse the soldier and it wasn't the young man's fault at all. Perhaps Anna had been casting an intoxicating cloud of perfume and sex in the soldier's direction ever since they met. But maybe it *was* the soldier's fault after all. The fact that he had put his arm around her earlier in the day was a dead give away. Certainly it had annoyed Anderson at the time, but in the context it wasn't yet strong enough evidence for him to act on, especially since he had resolved to be forgiving and understanding rather than petty and vengeful. But this laughter was different. It came from *her*. It bloomed forth from the most private recesses of her heart. It said something definite and in no way abstract, something about her innermost emotions and the way she felt about the soldier and how she yearned to get closer to him.

He listened to them for what seemed like an eternity. At one point she stood up and disappeared into the darkness only to come back about two minutes later to resume her seat directly beside the young man. It would have been a perfect opportunity to beak off the conversation and come to join Anderson, but she was obviously enjoying herself too much to give him so much as a thought as he sat there listening to them beneath the cold and chiseled light of the stars. Her voice became almost inaudible. Anderson surmised she was likely speaking about something deeply personal while possibly thinking about making love to the soldier beside the warm hiss and purr of the rising flames. Anderson struggled to hold himself back. On the chance that he was wrong, any confrontation would just be taken as an attempt to further destroy their marriage at a time when they needed one another the most. It was something she would never forgive, something she would bring up ten years later in a fight or use against him to gain some new foothold the very next time he let down his guard. The soldier was likely armed and might try to kill Anderson in the event of a showdown. And if this happened, the soldier might go crazy and end up killing Anna too. But what if the soldier just wanted to sleep with Anna and then shoot them both? Things like this appeared frequently enough in the newspapers, so why couldn't it also happen to them? As Anderson gradually sank into the world of sleep and forgetfulness, his last conscious thought was a voice of inner calm, even benediction, that said he was just being paranoid and the soldier was a decent righteous man just sharing some campfire tales with Anna and that he would be offended by any unwarranted accusation and might subsequently refuse to lead them through to Hungary. Then all was darkness.

V

The next morning Anderson awoke to find Anna sleeping beside him. His memories from the night before were vague and fragmented, like the incoherent mumblings of a drunk. The soldier's sleeping bag was rolled up neatly beneath a tall white fir tree, but he was nowhere in sight. The sky was filled with clusters of dark blue-gray clouds aligned in a rigid mesh-like pattern that stretched as far as the eye could see. Anderson heard the call of a heron too far away to pinpoint and then took a deep breath, savoring for a moment the feeling clean moist air in his lungs. He ran his finger through Anna's hair. She turned around and sniffled, her bright blue eyes shining like tiny pools springing from the snowy white bed of her face.

"I'm sorry," she said.

"For what?" Anderson asked.

"*What not for?* might be a better question."

"I'm sorry too," he said. For a moment he felt an opening between them, a dimly lit passage that led to the way things used to be between them. "I had a thought last night that scared me and made me think it wasn't worth it anymore."

She looked at him with a deep penetrating look that made him feel more young and vulnerable than he really was. Then she spoke:

"My mother always wanted me to be perfect – a person devoid of any flaws capable of mastering any subject or craft. I spent half my life trying to please her while at the same time desperately struggling to break away from her to become a person that was entirely an "I" without any roots in her desires. In so doing I ended up becoming something that was neither Anna nor what my mother wanted me to be. A kind of grotesque gargoyle of broken aspirations, other people's desires, and my own self loathing."

A heron cried a second time and then a strange rumbling filled the sky. It was far too cool and early in the day for a thunderstorm. It was probably the sound of a jet somewhere in the distance. Her words made him feel guilty for doubting her and convinced him that the affair was nobody's fault, but rather something uncontrollable and bad that happened at a time when uncontrollable and bad things were happening all around them; it was far less important in the grand scheme of things than either of them could ever really imagine and making too much of it was not only childish and narcissistic, but also painfully revealing of their own lack of insight and perspective.

"I've always been so selfish with you," he said. "Forever assuming your struggles were no more than a force directed at me as a way of getting back at me for not being the perfect husband."

She looked at him in a tender way that made him feel certain that all had been mended between them and that she had forgiven him for not really forgiving her and that their relationship was headed back to normal and might even take off in some new direction they hadn't yet explored – channeling towards some undiscovered island of understanding and tranquility. He felt for the first time that life was something both nurturing and ineffable, something like God, but even more loving and intangible.

"All we have to do is get to Hungary," he said with the solidity of a fire marshal, letting the words fall from his lips in soft but deliberate way. He remembered the first time they were in Budapest. It was two years before and she brought a small pinhole camera with her that she kept leaving behind in restaurants wherever they went. It was a city where the most amazing things could happen between two people, a place he always longed to return to. "Then everything will be good again."

Anderson heard the rustling of leaves and turned around to find the soldier standing there behind him. He was fully dressed and held a walking stick that he must have just picked up as Anderson hadn't noticed before.

"We have to get moving," the soldier said. "I know it is early but we have to move." He looked at Anderson for a moment before turning his gaze to Anna. "I heard the sound of jets. Maybe surveillance planes. They couldn't have been more than ten miles away. We have to avoid open areas to make sure they don't fly over and spot us."

The soldier went over to the pile of slate and took out a knife and started carving something into the ground. Anderson got out of his sleeping bag and then helped Anna out of hers. The sky was clear azure and a flock of geese passed overhead. They set off through the forest on the far side of the rock terrace and by noon were ascending a series of switchbacks that scaled the side of a small mountain. When they reached the summit they found themselves in a small open field speckled with half a dozen small deserted shacks arranged in a loose circle suggesting that a renegade battalion had once established a short-term base there. They hurried across the field to a slope that led down to an emerald colored lake couched in a natural bowl between three large peaks. By the time they reached the shore Anderson started to feel weak. He knelt down and took a deep breath, looking across the glassy waters of the lake at a flat-topped brick structure standing on the other side that looked like it might once have been used as a boathouse. The soldier picked up a stone and through it across the water. Anna clapped her hands as it skipped over the surface. The soldier clapped with her and then gave her a stone to try herself. She slipped as she threw it and the young man quickly grabbed her.

She looked at the soldier for a long moment before pulling away from his grasp. He had a look of intrusive self-confidence in his eyes, like an actor waiting tables in some modern themed restaurant in California. It was a face he had not yet shown to Anderson.

They walked along the shore of the lake until they came to the foot of one of the larger mountains on the other side.

"Four days more," said the soldier. "Then we will be in Virovitica." He said the name of the village with a sense of authority that hinted he had been there before and was looking forward to going back. "It's the last town before the border."

Anderson nodded his head in approval and turned to gauge Anna's reaction. She had a dreamy, almost fey look in her eyes that he found sensual. Was she thinking of the life they would have together once they escape? Or maybe she was thinking of some ancient city like Babylon or Ur where men in bronze armor worshipped outlandish stone idols – a secret world she had conjured up herself and had never revealed to anyone, not even him. This seemed plausible because when they lived back in New York she always used to read and reread Flaubert's "Salambo" for its lavish depiction of ancient ritual and dress.

By evening they had reached yet another lake and set up a small camp at a point where the water narrowed to form the mouth of a slow-moving river. As darkness fell Anderson was overcome with exhaustion. He helped the solider build a fire while Anna sat ten yards away stretching her legs and arms in makeshift Yoga positions. They shared what was left of the bread and cheese in Anna's backpack before Anderson laid out his sleeping bag and crawled inside.

"Sleeping?" Anna asked in a way that was pat, even impatient, as though she had been waiting all day for him to crawl into that sleeping bag and leave her alone.

"Yes," he said.

As he tried to force himself to sleep he became aware of the sound of crickets filling the air and every time he opened his eyes he was almost blinded by the milky wash of the stars overhead. There was an underlying tension in his body that prevented him from falling asleep. Just as he was about to fall asleep he became hyper-aware of his surroundings and heard - or imagined he had heard, he really wasn't sure – the soldier's voice speaking to Anna as they sat beside the fire.

Anna, when I first saw you I thought you were the most beautiful thing I had ever seen. You were supple, fresh, and warm in a way that made me feel like my life had changed and would never go back to the way it was before. I came from a small village and grew up in total silence. Everywhere was silence. Even when I was at home all I had was silence. Not even my mother or father would rescue me from it. At school they told me I was afraid to express myself. In the playground I was always standing alone wishing that someone would come up and join me. I grew up thinking I was nothing, the sort of person you would rather forget if you met me, or might not even remember in the first place. So, when I was eighteen, I joined the army. I thought by fighting for my country I would finally find that togetherness that I had always craved for. I thought by firing a weapon at an enemy I would empty myself of all my pain and anguish and become whole and pure again as I was at birth. As I was before my father got a hold of me and turned me into the person I was. As I was in the first instance. Yet now I find that everything has only become more complicated. When I killed my first man I felt nothing. There was no sense of victory. There was no severance. There was no purging. And out of the numbness that came over me grew only the flowers of guilt and self-hatred.

The fire breathed and crackled, filling the black night with an orange haze that seemed to envelope everything as rivulets of smoke and sparks floated upwards and vanished like fireflies into the darkness. Had he heard the soldier or was it only his imagination distorting the youth's words into some sinister and delusional soliloquy? He watched her through one open eye for the next ten minutes as she sat beside the soldier in apparent silence, their heads bowed down and facing each other like two people sharing a secret plan. From the distance her eyes looked wet. Maybe she felt something deep and profound for the soldier but was not yet ready to express herself. They were the same eyes that once met him in Prague on a bright June morning six months after they had first met, when she confessed that she loved him and could no longer live without him. They were the same bright eyes that drew him in and told him that he loved her as much as she did him and that he could not live without her.

She put her hand on the soldier's knee and squeezed it as though to reassure him. How could she? Anderson thought, anger and revulsion now simmering inside him. How could she after their conversation this morning? He heard a wolf howling in the distance and then something that sounded like an elk moaning from the other side of the lake. When the sounds faded to echoes and the echoes faded to silence he could once again hear the soldier's voice. This time it was muffled and slow, an artificial weight attached to every word. The voice slowly faded into nothingness and when Anderson was sure that all he could here was the faint ringing in his ears, a soft whispering he quickly attributed to Anna filled the air. In the darkness her voice rang out like a tiny bell, charming the faint orchestra of nighttime sounds with a sweet alluring call that made him at once long for her presence and detest her for not being by his side.

Just when Anderson was about to get out of his sleeping bag to confront them, she stood up and walked in his direction. When she stopped in front of him all he could see was her outline, traced in jittering orange light by the fire now twenty yards behind her.

"Are you asleep?" she asked without intonation.

"No," he said.

"I'm tired," she said. Then she slid into her sleeping bag, leaned over and kissed him on the cheek. "Good night," she said blankly, without a trace of deceit in her voice.

"Good night," he replied.

"You're not still angry, are you?"

"No," he said, although he was not sure he meant it.

Anderson cast his gaze towards the hearth. The soldier was playing with his knife as he stared wondrously into the fire. In the orange light of the flame he looked smaller than he really was, like a weak and vulnerable person who should not be sitting by himself in the middle of a great forest at night. The wind suddenly picked up and Anderson thought he heard an owl somewhere nearby. The sound of the owl faded and he saw a devilish white form undulating in the darkness at a point that could have been the top of a tree, but then it too faded before vanishing altogether. When he looked back at the hearth the soldier was gone. Anderson guessed he had gone to bed, and so turned his attentions to trying to locate the mysterious white form. It was likely the owl he had heard; he imagined its sharp beak and claws as it swooped down while everyone was asleep, creating havoc in its desperate search for food. But before he was able to spot the white form a second time, he was overcome with a feeling of immobility and stasis. His limbs felt numb and lifeless. Years later he would remember the feeling as he lay in his sleeping bag slowly passing over a threshold before losing complete consciousness of everything but the fact that he was falling away from the world. He entered a deep sleep that permeated every corner of his being. Although he didn't dream, several times he rose into a state of partial awareness of a world in which everything was evil and nothing could be touched without risking some form of contamination or spiritual decay. He fought against whatever unseen force was pushing him into this world, but to no avail. Whenever he struggled to pull away from this realm, he only found himself further enmeshed in its web of strange unearthly laws and perils.

When he finally opened his eyes, he turned to shake Anna's arm, but she was gone. Thinking that he had not yet awoke and the surroundings were just the landscape of another dream, he pinched his face before breaking out into a chorus of rebellious laughter. Then he shouted out a word he didn't know or understand – for all he knew it was part of a foreign language and his mind was being controlled by some hidden force – in an act of defiance against whoever or whatever it was that was making him dream. But when he heard the wind howling he knew he was awake.

He crept out of his sleeping bag and walked over to the fire. There was no sign of anyone. He walked over to the soldier's sleeping bag and again there was no one. There was a sudden pop from the dying embers and he then became aware of an echo from the mountain peaks overhead. For an instant he thought it was a human voice, but as it repeated and gradually died down he realized it was something non-human, something like a falling rock or minor avalanche that was distorted by the hills and mountain peaks into something vaguely human and almost recognizable.

An invisible switch flicked on inside him; his mind focussed on his immediate surroundings. Anna was gone. And so was the soldier. He imagined them off in some intimate mountain hideaway making love in soft and uncontrollable gasps as they watched the moonlight reflect off the surface of the nearby lake while lying in a cold dewy bed of overgrown grass. He imagined her wet skin and the expression on her face as she made love. Was it one of passion or one of revenge? If it was one of revenge, what was she avenging? But maybe she really was in love with the soldier and was helpless to do anything as he lured her into his arms. As the embers lost their color and faded into darkness, he started to feel sorry for Anna for being so weak. She was obviously a gentle and misguided creature, a woman who fell victim over and over again to her urges to help others and make them happy. He heard another pop, but this time from behind him in the forest, and another thought entered his head. If she really was so weak and overly altruistic with her affections, why was she not showing the same sympathy for him? Had he simply overspent his due and was their conversation that morning just her way of saying goodbye?

Anderson kicked his foot into the dirt and walked closer to the hearth where the light from the dying embers had suddenly intensified and begun to pulse in shades of red and yellow, punctuated by nodes of total darkness as it emitted a glow just large enough to create a glowing dome of color about five feet in radius. He sat down and waited. He heard a rustling in the bushes and stood up for a moment. But when he heard the wind moaning like some kind of strange Arabic wind instrument, he sat down. What he was sure was a living being lurking in the darkness behind the bushes was nothing but the natural flow of air through the forest.

He stood up again and then reached down to pick up a heavy stick for protection. He would have to go and look for them and it was best to go armed. Not only was there the chance he might confront some random assailant – a mountain lion or band of renegade soldiers looking for victims – but there was always the possibility that if he found the soldier, alone or with Anna, he would fire at Anderson and not just because he thought Anderson was a mountain lion or enemy infantry. He knelt down beside his sleeping bag, which he could barely make out under the light of the stars, moon, and dying embers of the fire, and reached down to the bottom where he immediately felt the smooth wooden surface touching his fingertips. He grabbed it and squeezed it, sensing in his palm which end was the best to hold and which the best to brandish. Tightening his hand around the shaft until it settled tightly in his palm, he thrust it forward into the darkness of the night.

He went first to the shore of the lake. Calling her name was out of the question as it might leave him open to attack. He watched the light glitter off the surface like candlelight off a thousand jewels in an elegant ballroom. He was seized by a sudden sense of outrage. Why was he standing there looking for the very woman who should be begging him to take her back after everything she had done? Weren't they just taking him for a fool? He felt for a moment like he did in his recurring dream where he is standing in the middle of a restaurant with hundreds of high-ranking literati who had all read his book and found it dreadful and pretentious. He was small and insignificant, no more important than any one of the blades of light dancing like swords across the surface of the lake. He had given her enough chances. Nobody could deny it. And besides, hadn't their love always been defined as one of him coming to her? It was a motion of the male to the female and never the other way around. It was a flux, but a flux in only one direction. Whenever they argued, it was up to him to decide they had enough and try to apologize and set things off in a fresh and more constructive direction. But when he first came to her he was a man looking for a woman who could settle him down and pull him together. Without him she was still whole and pure while without her, he was incomplete and unfinished like a sketch of a some potentially great painting that needed an artist's hand to pick up a brush and guide it to fruition. For the first time since he met her, the image of a beautiful woman - that wasn't Anna - sitting in his living room engaged him for long enough to make him wonder if he had made a mistake by marrying her. Was it possible that he would be better off with someone else?

He exhaled and stepped backwards from the water. He walked back to his sleeping bag. He straightened it on both sides and rolled it up the best he could in the dim light. Then he grabbed his backpack and walked back to the lake. For what seemed like an eternity he sat beside a log on the shore in complete silence until the first rays of dawn became visible as long pink shafts rising like columns from the mountains in the distance. When the sun appeared from behind the mountains he started walking along the side of the lake in a direction he knew was north, calculating in his mind how long it would take to reach the other end and then after that how much longer it would take for him to reach the Hungarian border. Now he was truly alone.

Part II

58

I

Anderson clenched his fist as he crunched his way through a patch of frosted grass, turning away from a small diamond-shaped briar patch as he made his way further and further from the lake, and therefore Anna and the soldier. It was now clear to him that she had chosen to leave him long ago and all she was waiting for was the right guy to come along and whisk her away and she had only come back to him as a part of a holding pattern in her quest to find someone new. Without the soldier it might take him longer to get to the border, but as long as he moved northeast by the stars until he found the next road he could use his map to guide him in the right direction. There would also be fewer Serbian troops on the mountain and to the north, so for the time being he felt safe. He crossed a small brook the surface of which was dimpled by leaves and tiny insects and carved in random furrows made by the westward breeze. He stopped for a moment to watch a small grouping of flower petals the size of his thumbnail move slowly downstream. They swirled through an eddy to a portion of the river whose waters were so clear he could almost make out the reflection of the Roman viaduct rising up from behind a grove of trees on a nearby hill, the morning sun casting a burnished glow across its smooth and sloping arches. Following its shimmering image to the edges of the water and then to the ground directly in front of him, he spotted an unusual stone the shape of an arrow lying beside his right foot. He leaned over to pick it up, studying the vague outlines of what looked like a fossil of a prehistoric shrimp-like creature on the side. The past had a way of making its indelible mark.

The first time he left Anna was six years ago. They had just come back from a Manhattan party to honor a well-respected journalist named Ned Barker who had just won a Jewish literary prize neither of them had ever heard of. He and Anna had too much to drink and ended up leaving early. He could still remember the reflection of the light from the street lamp off her large wet eyes as they walked home. She was wearing a thin embroidered sweater and kept chewing on a toothpick she had been rolling between her fingers since they left the party. When they got back to their Lower West Side apartment they sat down on the couch in the living room and immediately started kissing. After a failed attempt at making love - in the middle of which he broke out laughing and admitted he had *a bad case of whiskey dick* and was far too drunk to go any further - they picked up fragments of a conversation that had been bandied about at the party and started arguing about twentieth-century art. For the next half hour he insisted that Jasper Johns was a better artist than August Renoir – a view she angrily claimed he had borrowed from his first girl friend, a German exchange student he met as a freshman in college. He had never seen her so jealous before. It was completely out of character. He put on his coat to leave and she stood up and threw a glass at him. It hit the side of his face and careened off to hit the wall, leaving a deep indentation the shape of a crescent directly beneath a black-and-white photo of her as a three year old playing with a bucket of sand. Instead of retaliating, he just shook his head in disgust – more at their mutual drunkenness than anything in her personality or behavior – and walked out the door into the late-night rain. By the time he was half a block away she had already caught up to him. With her wet hair and long pink nightgown, also wet and clinging to her cold willowy body, she looked like a lost Victorian child in need of help. Without a thought he embraced her, protecting her from whatever dangers – real or only imagined, lurking invisibly inside her - the night might hold. They walked back to their apartment, for the moment ignoring, even enjoying the rain, swearing that they loved each other more than anything and arguments like this would never happen again.

The second time he walked out on her was almost exactly two years later. She was playing the violin and refused to come to bed. As the night wore on, the pieces grew more and more fierce, colder and more disjointed in their style. His first thought was that she was angry at something distant and abstract in her life that had nothing to do with him, and because of this he sympathized with her. But the longer she played the more he was convinced that it was something in himself she was attacking. When he finally got out of bed to talk to her she pretended he wasn't even in the room at all and just continued playing. At one point she put the violin down right in the middle of an aria and looked right at him as though he were a piece of furniture of part of the wall. So he threw on his clothes, grabbed his coat, and walked down the hall and through the door into the cool New York night. When he got to the closest bar he sat down and ordered a scotch and opened a tab. But by his third double he was overcome with guilt for abandoning her without making the slightest effort to understand her behavior. He paid for his drinks and when he got home she was lying in bed smiling calmly as though nothing had happened. They made love with quiet intensity and the incident was never mentioned again.

This was the third time he left her. As he ascended to the peak of a small hill, enjoying a panoramic view of the rising sun on the horizon when he reached the top, he was overcome by a grave premonition that this time there would be no easy solution. This time whatever damage had already been done was irreversible. He felt torn inside as he made his way down the hill. In abandoning Anna had he not also violated and sinned against the young woman he met one magical summer in Switzerland and eventually took back with him to America? By doing so wasn't he also negating his past and destroying everything his life's history had been founded on? The book that was Anderson now had missing chapters and other chapters that had to be torn out and rewritten. Somewhere inside the confused adulteress she had somehow become – he imagined her making love to the soldier, with a cold and vengeful face, as the dawn broke over the mountain peak and cast its silvery rays across the surface of the lake – was still a trace of that wondrous ball of light and warmth he had once fallen in love with. Was it possible to defend yourself by not attacking anybody at all – not even your opponent - and in so doing become the aggressor? He conceded that he didn't know and as he inhaled the fragrant mountain air he wondered if he ever would. Perhaps it wasn't really man's place at all to ever know anything about himself and the world. All things had their place in life. All things had their home. And when things strayed far enough away from their natural place, was not Man opening himself up to all manner of peril? As a shark was not meant to hunt in the sand, perhaps it was man's position not to know anything about himself or others – nothing at all – and coming to terms with this without any regret or expectation was the only real way to happiness.

He walked past a row of stubby evergreen trees that seemed to form a natural wall between his current path and a large field that spread out into the gray and formless distance. The landscape was the very antithesis of beauty and love. He toyed with the thought that the field, in standing as a metaphor for what his life had become with Anna, was a message from some ineffable guardian or divine communicator that he had done the right thing and was free to move on. How could he have been so trusting and naïve to never see the truth? In the first few months after he met her, their relationship was a ecstatic composite of café meetings rolling cigarettes from crude French tobacco as though characters in Goddard's *Masculine Feminine* and long telephone conversations about "European things", in the words of Jonathan Richman's *Modern Lovers*, things like Lou Reed, David Bowie, and the so-called *Berlin three* – with a few random sexual encounters at places as far afield from one another as the rare book collection at the city library and the rooftop of his apartment building. But for some reason these encounters – however spontaneous and passionate they were – had never impacted him as much as the phone conversations. That was what really won him over. Those long minutes with only the sound of her sniffling as he waited for her to answer. If Heraclitus once said that *everything was fire*, could this not also include his telephone conversations with Anna? He stepped around a small bush and tossed a rock beside it, recalling a time he once talked with her on the telephone about an article he had read in *The New York Times* describing a new trend in parts of Manhattan where people explored secret passages in abandoned subway stations (Penn Station and Union Square were ones that stood out in his mind) claiming that these inner bowels of the city were the last frontier in the world and by exploring this facet of modern life the practitioners had become like the great explorers of the nineteenth century or the soul-searching French symbolist poets of the same period. The conversation went on for two or three hours, eventually leading to a discussion on whether or not it was really possible to love another person at all and how this was the underlying theme of Bach's suites for violin cello, although neither of them were able to say exactly why they believed this. Finally, when both of them were too tired to come up with anything new to talk about, they said goodnight and hung up the phone in unison.

By mid morning he reached the lip of a small glacier that spilled down the side of a tall mountain like a tongue from the mouth of giant dog. The ice was white on the surface but still transparent in a way that made it look bluer in areas where it seemed to run more deep than others. In the distance he could see a small church standing isolated in the middle of a ring of tall trees. It was the first building he had seen since leaving the village and it made him feel secure, his second sign to reassure him that he had made the right choice in leaving Anna behind – as if he needed reassurance at all, as it was really Anna and the soldier that had abandoned him! The church had an air of invitation about it, almost demanding him to step forward and take part in whatever its presence on earth had to offer. Beyond the church there was a narrow brook that stretched out in myriad directions like a cluster of small blue veins on the leg of an older woman. The scene had the look of a medieval icon with its almost perfect depiction of depth through the geometric vehicle of the winding stream receding from the foreground to the background. He crossed the small glacier and made his way across a field to the church. The outside walls were covered with graffiti in a language he didn't recognize, the unknown words arranged like crawling like vines around four stained glass windows, two on either side of the front entrance. Like most of the churches in Croatia, it was dull and colorless on the outside and arranged in a cruciform design, the front entrance situated at the base of the cross. He opened the door and stepped inside. The floor of the central aisle was covered with ashes and broken furniture; half-burnt dolls and kitchen appliances were strewn across the floor. Strangely, the pews were perfectly intact and showed no sign of damage or misuse. It was as though someone had come all the way from a nearby village with the sole purpose of dumping the last remnants of their furniture, wrecked and burned in a military attack, in the center aisle to defile the church. The altar was also in perfect order, a wine glass standing in the middle. He picked it up and examined the dark stains inside, gathered together in concentric rings that spread out from a central point above the stem as though the glass had been left filled with wine and allowed to evaporate.

Satisfied that there was nothing in the wreckage or by the altar that could help him, he walked back outside where a soft rain had cast a rainbow haze over the field to the north. He continued walking until the rain became so intense it became a scourge of sharp pins thrust into his head and face. He stopped under a bushy tree and waited until the rain slowed to a drizzle. Then he walked until he came upon a deep forest lined with slender blue-green fir trees. The trail he followed into the dense wood seemed angled upwards as though ascending the side of a hill he could not see was there, so with every stride he had to relieve the strain on his back by leaning forward, sometimes cupping his palm over his knee to support the weight of his upper body. As the sun began to set he broke away from the forest into a small glade, a cluster of bushes standing in the center. It was a perfect place to rest and possibly set up his sleeping bag for the night. The bushes were far enough away from the boundary of the forest for safety from nocturnal predators, yet they also provided enough natural shelter to protect him from a storm if one happened to come.

He reached into his bag and pulled out a piece of stale bread. Although it was the last of his food, it was best to eat it before it got any worse and worry about getting more later. Live for the moment. He took a hesitant bite. That was one thing Anna had always taught him. She was the kind of person that lived primarily to enjoy herself and only took care of problems as they came along. Before they met he was always studying, focused on finishing his studies with high enough standing to get a dream job at a newspaper in some perfect city, yet she made him realize how much he had wasted his youth in an effort to make this dream come true. *Say you get a job in your ideal city and you find out that in the process of working to get that job you have changed so much that it is no longer your ideal city and because of this you are not happy, yet you lived the last five years in a cave shutting out the rest of the world so nothing could distract you from your ultimate goal.* But no matter how wise were her words, everything was different now. In leaving her behind with the soldier – or, more accurately, his reaction to them leaving him behind - he had shown her once and for all that he didn't need her advice and could go forward in life without her.

When he finished the bread he was overcome by a sense of exhaustion. The sun was sinking below the peak of a nearby mountain – now just visible through a space in the forest canopy - as though to signal that it was permissible for him to end the day and fall asleep. He removed his backpack and unrolled the red and white down-filled sleeping bag, smoothing it flat against the ground with both his hands. Then he took off his pants and climbed in, taking pride in the fact that it was the end of his first full day away from Anna in almost two years. He was surprised that he did not miss her as much as he thought he would; any trace of guilt he might have felt for not trying harder to find her and the soldier was completely absent. She had decided to leave him for the soldier and she had to live with that choice for the rest of her life, for better or for worse. Perhaps she wanted Anderson to hunt her down and challenge the soldier to a duel, a figurative sword fight with their cocks, in order to prove his worth. But in the wake of her previous affair why would he even bother?

When he closed his eyes he felt happy to finally relax and loosen his grip on the world. In sleep lived all those things one couldn't find in daily life. It was a world of the imagination where thoughts could freely move unbound by rules or objectives. To be creative by day meant work, yet in sleep the same artistic impulses could flow without the burden of aspirations to the material, something like a book or statue that was the marriage of the physical and the mental in a way that compromised both.

He fell asleep almost immediately. As the night wore on he awoke several times, as much aware of a soft wind passing over his face as he was of his new found freedom, yet each time he momentarily rose from the depths of his slumber he was as quickly pulled downwards again into a state in which he was conscious of nothing. When dawn came he opened his eyes just once before closing them again and observing himself from some hovering psychological vantage point as he lay in the middle of a glade dreaming. For what seemed like several years or even a lifetime – he had no grasp of time other than the fact that the world in which he existed was an alternate to his daily world and had different rules of permanence and history – he was able to fly over a number of small villages, only occasionally landing on a castle wall or before the doors of a subway station connecting the villages by way of a complex series of tunnels. Although he had no wings his ability to fly seemed natural and stemmed from an inner emotional effort as opposed to an exterior physical effort. All he had to do was concentrate and focus the right set of feelings inside him and he could fly as high as he wanted over any landscape. Yet this proved to be harder than he had originally thought, as several times he suddenly dropped ten or fifteen feet and almost hit the top of a telephone pole or roof of a building. The emotions required to move upwards were ones of awe and exhilaration that were difficult to sustain without some external stimulus to inspire them. If his mind lost focus for just an instant, these feelings would wane, causing him to lose momentum and nosedive towards the ground. Eventually he grew tired of flying and decided to explore the subways. The air was for clouds, birds, and flying insects and although beautiful, it lacked a certain human element that made him crave contact with other people. In the time frame of this dream he was still with Anna, so his first thought as he started his descent was where he could go to find her, although this seemed awkward because part of him knew it was only a dream and that they were no longer together. Even so, the subways seemed like an obvious place to find her. When he landed he entered a subway station and took a downward escalator, riding it past a series of posters advertising the same circus event in myriad ways – each one different and more unsettling than the last in its depiction of deformed and hideous performers: a man with the head of a rhinoceros; a woman with three arms, snails crawling from inside her mouth; a man with no eyes and a neck as thin as a teaspoon. The subway platform was filled with nameless and grotesque people, reading books or staring at their watches as though they were too wrapped up in their own worlds to notice him. A train pulled up to the platform and when he boarded he noticed an ad for a book, his own name spelled out in large block letters beneath the title. Beside it was an ad for a new soft drink. Apparently in this world his dream-book was a success and not the butt end of disparaging remarks at pretentious restaurants and literati hangouts. He looked closer at the ad, which now seemed composed of undulating passages, the words of which he could never quite discern before they vanished and transformed into other, equally mysterious verbal objects and symbols. As they pulled away from the station he became aware that the rhythm of the undulating words was intimately tied to that of his breathing pattern, inclining him to think that the book was much greater than any text, an expression of the very essence of his soul in living and breathing color. If this was true, then weren't all those nameless, faceless people, many of whom must have read his book if it was important enough to be advertised on a subway train, able to access his deepest inner feelings with just as much facility as one would read the sports column of a morning paper? The thought disturbed him so much that he had to hold himself back from hitting a man in the face who was standing next to him smoking a pipe, a copy of Anderson's soul-book poking out of his jacket pocket. Anderson got off at the next stop and when the doors of the train closed he looked back at the man with the pipe and noticed his face had changed to resemble that of Anna. The man's chin was smooth and rounded without being plump and he had the same deep-set blue eyes and slightly puckered mouth. In desperation he tried to wave, but it was too late. The train was already in motion and Anna was nowhere in sight. With a great gasp he tried calling out for her but instead woke up cold and sweating in a sleeping bag in the middle of a forest with only the memory of having just screamed loudly. Moments later he was back asleep, but this time the darkness afforded by sleep brought nothing but deep and prolonged silence.

When he awoke for good he had no idea what time it was, but the sun was already a third of the way across the sky. As he gathered together his things and prepared for the day's journey he reflected on the meaning of the dream. There was something significant in the depiction of the book. It was the first time it had ever been shown in a dream as anything vaguely successful. This was a good sign. But successful to whom? Although the people in the dream were grotesque, it was still a world that gave him free license to fly, and he doubted whether any of the people in the subway had such privileges. Was he doomed to be a prince in a land of people he had no kinship with or liking for?

He set off northwards through a shallow marsh filled with tall cattails swaying gently in the midday breeze. Perhaps the appearance of Anna's face was a form of hidden guilt rising to the surface and finally making its stand. It was the kind of thing she would do. Have an affair and then run off with a soldier when things were just starting to look good and then turn around and try to make him feel guilty for retaliating.

The scent of some kind of wild animal filled the air and a feeling of preternatural lightness came over him – the same sensation he remembered from the dream while he was flying – as he crossed a small brook. A sudden breeze gusted against his face, transporting him to an imagined scene in which he was alone on a dock looking out at the ocean; the rays of the sun against his face were like small, loving hands caressing his soul. The Hungarian border couldn't be more than a few days ahead of him and all he had to grasp was a future, a future without Anna that would be completely his to explore. He closed his eyes and opened them again in a metaphoric act of death and renewal.

As he walked northwards through a field evenly interspersed with small pine trees and clumps of wet grass he became more and more confident with his decision to leave Anna. Why had he given so much of his life to her? It seemed all those years he was like a man standing in an empty room playing air guitar to music blaring on his headphones, living life in a closed shell of his own making and experiencing things in the outer world only by proxy. It wasn't that he hadn't experienced anything – how could one even suggest that of a man escaping by himself across a treacherous mountain range in the midst war-torn Yugoslavia? - but rather that by virtue of him being so attached to her he had never experienced mature adult existence as a fully fledged individual. His day-to-day life with her in New York and more recently in Croatia, while rife with endless interviews, appointments, and dinner engagements with various politicians and local businessmen, was little more than a host of illusions. He was a modern day Prospero, living on some abandoned desert island of the soul surrounding himself with a world of illusion. Even his recent escape from Pozega was something done *with her*. So while grandchildren on his knee decades in the future might think his tale of averting Serbian troops was as daring and adventurous as a fictional pirate story, it was still done *with her* and because of this it was not a *true* experience, but rather just a steppingstone on the way to becoming a fully seasoned human being.

The sun moved higher into the sky as he continued across the lumpy field and towards a hilly region where small boulders gathered on the base of each slope. On the ground were scattered red and blue flowers with broad rounded petals and tall rigid stems. He had never seen this species before and wondered if it was indigenous to the area or had been transplanted there in some days past by some kind of Serbian Marco Polo who traveled across the world in search of exotic flora. He inhaled deeply, enjoying a certain musky scent in the air. Was it connected to the strange unearthly blue and red flowers? As he made his way up a small incline, the thought occurred to him that Anna had entered his life to teach him how to be whole and complete, and now that he had finally mastered her cleverly disguised regimen of life lessons he was free to face life in a new and dynamic way, so neither of them had any reason to harbor any bitterness over their break up.

II

Anderson made his way up a steep hill and stopped when he reached its crest. On the other side, almost lost in a bed of mist at the base of the valley below, stood a small village, the rooftops of a few of its tallest buildings gradually emerging into view; a few chimneys and then a steeple poked through the cloud-like layer without revealing a trace of the base structures below and so appeared like independent objects floating in some vast embryonic ocean. The dream-like landscape seemed to suggest in metaphoric terms *the past* or *personal history*, and thus conjured forth images of Anna and the soldier laughing about how much of a fool Anderson was for straggling away from them - the core of the escape party - at a time of such duress. Maybe they even thought he was dead. "Let her think that," he muttered as he stumbled downwards towards the ghost-like village. If anything, the truth was the exact opposite. *Rumors of my death are grossly exaggerated*, he said to himself, repeating Mark Twain's words over and over in his head, savoring the details of their irony, which seemed to grow with nuance and expand with every cycle of repetition. The strong overstatement *grossly exaggerated* was used in such a way that it came across as a clever understatement, since a person is either dead or alive and never in between, and so such a matter was not something that could be exaggerated, which would imply the existence of degrees of death or life. But perhaps Twain was really suggesting that there *were* degrees of life and death and you could be half dead when you really thought you were alive, and this was yet another layer of meaning.

Whatever the case, Anderson was more alive than ever. Perhaps it was the effect of time, but he was already starting to feel more removed and philosophical about his break up with Anna. There was nothing like perspective to put things in order. He made his way through a series of switchbacks down towards the village, thinking of all the ways his life would change once he made it back to New York. He could start his own magazine as he had always wanted. All it would take was a small business loan and a downtown office and he'd be off to the races. Days he would work as a writer and publisher, striving to become a world-renowned literary presence through a series of short stories and perspectives rather than the workaday journalist he had been previously, while at night he could start by listening to his stereo and finally reading in depth the hundreds of novels he had bought in used bookstores over the years but never had the time to pick up, and later, after most people had gone to bed, he would go out to restaurants and nightclubs where he could meet all kinds of interesting people – *half of them women.* Anna may have been the right girl for him during his younger years, but he was clearly a different man now. Not that he would ever love anyone as much as Anna – that was impossible – but things with Anna had clearly run their course and it was time to try out a different type of woman. But maybe in this new phase of life there was no one woman that would suit all his needs and he would lead the life of a playboy, enjoying casual liaisons with hip New York artists and career women alike, all mature and independent enough to recognize that what they were sharing together was something beautiful, made even more so because of the transitory nature of their affair. Although he had always thought he was the type to love only once, perhaps a new John Anderson, more dynamic and daring than the old one, had been hibernating inside him all along just waiting for a chance to break free and express itself. As he stumbled over a small rock, he reveled in the image of this new man standing in front of a Fifth Avenue restaurant kissing an exuberant red head in the style of

Monica Vitti - dressed in a long white overcoat, held loosely at the waist by a thick matching belt as the wind blew through her hair and she repositioned her sun glasses on her nose. Yes, he thought as he broke into a light gallop towards the gathering of angled rooftops partially buried in the bed of clouds below, he had a lot to look forward to now that he was finally free.

Of course, Anna would always be a major part of his life. There was no question of this. Once the dust settled they would make up and become friends in the same way Sartre and Simone de Beavoire had been, bound together by a force much stronger than either of them would ever admit. They would meet every few weeks for lunch to exchange morsels of gossip and wisdom about their respective personal affairs. What would she say to him about the soldier the next time they met? Where would it be? A restaurant in Paris? A castle in Ireland? An intimate seacoast hideaway in Santa Barbara? Would she expect him to be the same? Would she recount to him every sordid detail of her romance with the soldier? His mind reeled with countless possibilities, all of them too far-fetched to visualize without a trace of a grin on his face.

He walked down a clay path, worn in the center to a bed of slate beneath the white and powdery cover layer of dust, past a grove of conifers and then through a sparsely wooded area speckled with thin black-trunked trees covered with light green leaves the size and shape of almonds, appearing almost translucent in the light of the sun. As he neared the rising bed of steeples and rooftops he could see further and further into the layer of mist from which they arose. Soon he could make out the beginnings of windows, some with awnings or shutters and others completely bare with nothing to screen them from the rays of the sun. There were also brick houses – in a style he had never seen before in this part of the country - suggesting that the village may have once been occupied for long enough for substantial building to occur – as well as other houses built of stone or wood that had been plastered over and then painted. When he reached the edge of the village he could make out a clock tower in what looked like a central square and beside that was a statue of a man riding a horse. Upon entering the village he noticed small clouds of mist gathering around him, giving the impression that he was descending into a netherworld in which different physical laws applied. The village was completely unoccupied as though some holocaust had come and gone, freezing all passage of time in its wake. This was a place where a man would get lost and never find himself again. A person could spend a lifetime here compiling and honing a final list of life's deepest truths only to find out he had instead compiled instead a list of complete falacies with no value to anyone, not even himself.

Just beyond an old gas station stood a sign with something written on it in a language he didn't recognize. It looked like some form of Latvian or Old Prussian by the strange markings above and below the letters and the overabundance of the letter S at the ends of words. He had once heard from an old Parisian man he met on a park bench in Nice that that the French didn't know how to pronounce half the village names in their own country because most of them were words that originated with the Celts or other peoples who occupied the land long before the Romans. About fifty yards from the sign was a small barn with a red door and beyond that was a building that looked like a church, but not the one with the steeple he had seen earlier. As he got closer he was able to make out a number of small cross-shaped windows on the front wall, and directly above them an odd hexagonal window, spindles of wood radiating from a center point. The collection of windows reminded him of houses he had once seen in New England, yet for a reason he couldn't quite pinpoint there was also something about them that reminded him of an apartment he once stayed across the road from in Prague. He was there for a few weeks one summer to cover an international trade meeting and write a feature article on tourism in Eastern Europe. Every morning he used to pass the same apartment on his way to a bus station where he would buy a cappuccino at a small kiosk from a short girl ash-blonde girl who always wore a black hair net and two rings on her wedding finger. She looked too young to be married and so he guessed she was just wearing the rings in service to some idiosyncratic fashion trend or perhaps to ward off unwanted suitors.

At night he could often see through his window across the lamp lit street into this apartment. Although the glare from the street was usually enough to obscure his view, he counted three people living inside – two men and one girl. Was she the same one from the kiosk? One of the men seemed to have a closer, although possibly not sexual, relationship with the woman while the other seemed to take the role of an onlooker, casually standing back and commenting on whatever they did together. He had never seen the three of them together in the street, although he once spotted the woman leaning out the window shouting something, her long sylphine hair and pale almost blue-white complexion immediately striking him as uncommonly beautiful, as though she were some fey nature spirit hovering over the world to rail against its injustices; she was clearly not the same girl who sold him cappuccino every morning! Although he was only going on a hunch, he strongly believed that the girl and male with whom she was more intimate were both addicted to heroin and that they were once lovers, their years of involvement with the drug slowly eroding every vestige of their sexual desire until there was no longer any strong romance between them. The reason he believed this was because there were always a few used needles lying on the street directly below the window in the morning. He had also once seen them standing naked together by the window, seeming absorbed in the melting by match flame some substance in a spoon. The second male figure was somewhat of a mystery, but Anderson suspected that he was a mutual friend who dabbled in drugs but didn't do heroin. He possessed a more wholesome, yet somehow still detached, look about him - like a sophomore of theology at a medieval seminary. Although Anderson had just started seeing Anna at the time, she was back in Switzerland, and so he often found himself daydreaming, sometimes for hours, about the girl in the apartment and what might happen if they one day met by chance on the street. In some fantasies he made love to her in the apartment while the other two sat watching them while in others he saved her from her drug addiction and freed her from her enslavement by the other two men.

A week before he left to go back to America an ambulance pulled up and took the girl away. The cherry and blue light of the white vehicle reflected off the puddles of rain on the street as the doors closed and the engines turned on, emitting a high-pitched drone that was just loud enough to drown out the sound of the imaginary crying in his head. He never found out what happened, and she did not return to the apartment for the remainder of his stay in Prague. In his mind he always linked her to Eurydice, as she seemed to posses some an otherworldly charm that was more than just superficially linked to his concept of death.

For the next few weeks every time he made love with Anna something inside him recounted this woman and how she might have died that night and what she must have felt those final moments of her life. Thoughts of her transformed from his initial sexual fantasies to images of suffering, spiritual purification, and transfiguration. As the months passed, he began to equate his sexual encounters with Anna with the actions of some abstract dictatorial power conjured in his mind out of unconscious guilt for not having saved the woman while he had the chance. Every time he so much as embraced Anna he felt he was exploiting her. It was more than a year before this feeling subsided, but soon after it reemerged transformed into virulent hatred towards anything related to domination, nationalism, or intolerance. Perhaps this was why he was always drawn to the smaller more unassuming countries of Europe rather than places like Germany, France and England, places that prickled with foul illusions of cultural superiority. It was in countries like Estonia – where he had once been for a few days to visit an old friend who had married a woman from Tartu – and now Croatia that would forever conjure forth thoughts of the woman in the window, her starlit eyes staring out into the night in a gaze of innocent sexuality, and it was in this ghostly village now at this very moment that images of her in his mind were suddenly more vivid and intense than any day since she disappeared in the ambulance. He took a few steps forward, his feet pressing deeply into a bed of wet leaves. Was he not like the interviewed man in *Citizen Kane* who thought Rosebud was the name of a girl that Kane had once loved or only seen? The same man then claimed he passed a woman on a street corner ten years earlier and that not a day had passed since that moment in which he didn't think of her at least once.

When he reached the town square he knelt beside the statue of the man on horseback and set down his backpack. There was a sudden darkness in the air as though a storm was coming, but when he looked up to the sky he couldn't see through the umbrella of overhanging mist. On street level there was no sign of life and everything had the eerie silence of a trap. He wondered if it was safe to stay in the village. Just as he was about to pick up his backpack and retrace his steps, he was overcome by a sudden pang of hunger. Perhaps it was a better idea to look for food, since he might not get another chance before reaching the border. He walked over to what looked like a café or restaurant. There might be a freezer inside still stocked with something edible. He inched slowly towards the yellow door, white arabesques hanging in relief on either side, and opened it. The light in the front room was dim. A smell, at once sweet and virulent, permeated the air. In entering the building, had he not just crossed a boundary into a completely different world? *Folyo* was the Hungarian word for river and *folyoso* was the word for corridor and *folyik* the verb meaning to continue. His crossing of the threshold was not only a physical action, but something much greater. He had once read that physicists developed the concept density of states to measure the concentration of continuous electronic states *flowing* through a metal; was this model also applicable to life? Was it possible to compress experience, feeling, and the connections between memories and the present in such a way as to intensify one's level of being or existence? Had he spent his life drawing experiences inward and hoarding them like some wicked jeweler rather than assimilating them and then spreading them outwards into the world to broaden or enrich the lives of people around him?

He walked past a row of chairs and tables and turned on a light switch. A fat bearded man was lying dead on the floor beside him with a knife sticking out of his stomach. In the corner, balanced on a stool and head face first on the wooden bar, was a second body, a man apparently shot in the act of drinking from the carton of milk still held firmly in his right hand. Another man, thinner than the first two, was lying dead on the ground, wrapped inside a thick green parka as though having just returned from a mountain expedition. There was a pistol in his hand. Anderson knelt down and touched the man's head. The skin was cold and stiff like a car seat in winter. He tried to lift the arm of the cadaver, but it was too rigid to move without risking breakage. He carefully wrested the gun from the dead man's hand and checked to see if it was loaded. It was. Hand gripped tightly around its wood-and-black-metal butt, he cast a darting glance behind him. Maybe there was a gunman still lurking somewhere inside the restaurant. As he backed out the front door he noticed for the first time, spray-painted on the far wall over a number of nude pin up posters ripped out of a magazine, the words "Die Croatian Scum". Directly below these words an abstract geometric symbol scribbled in pen took on the form of an eagle perched on a throne; it lunged out at him from the wall into the very fabric of the room, taking possession of his every idea and feeling like some kind of self-declared viceroy of destruction.

The mist had cleared and the sun was glaring down like a heat lamp as he inched out of the room, moving slowly away and backwards from the building. A crippling feeling like sickness or unimaginable loss came over him. He was nothing and the world was also nothing. His scalp was itchy and his chest was wet with sweat. He turned and crept northwards towards a church, its rustic steeple – maybe the one he had seen from the top of the hill – stretching skyward; abstract designs, too fine and intricate for him to fully discern, were engraved on its side, spanning as high as the cross gleaming at its very pinnacle.

He circled around to the back of the church. There was a small graveyard, knee-high gravestones standing in perfect rows about two meters apart with Latin inscriptions carved on their flat granite fronts. Beyond the graveyard a stone wall, lined on either side by a row of what looked like chestnut trees, rose from the dirt. He walked solemnly through the middle of the graveyard back to the garden, watching the patterns cast on the ground by the sunlight passing through the trees. He stopped in the middle of the graveyard at the front edge of a large shadow spanning outwards from behind a large tree to his left. The shadow was longer and darker than those cast by the branches of the trees, suggesting the presence of an unseen figure hidden somewhere behind the leaves. There was a gust of wind and the air was filled with a sound like the soft clapping of a hushed audience after the completion of some suite or symphonic movement. As he neared the stone wall, his eyes followed the shadow back to an object hanging about fifty feet in front of him and behind a tree. At first he thought it was a sack of clothing, but when he got closer the rounded features of a woman crystallized before his eyes. She was hanging from a noose, her long blonde hair fell across her face and down to her shoulders as it glistened in the sun. The wind blew again and her body swung gently back and forth like a grotesque pendulum used to mark the passing of the day. He brushed her hair aside, hoping to find some clue that her death was accidental and not as brutal as it seemed, but her neck was not broken and her grey peasant dress was covered with bloody pinholes: certain evidence that her death was slow and agonizing.

He stepped backwards from the swaying body. The air was thick and noxious, almost too heavy to breath. The wind, once a chime, became a death knell. The branches of the chestnut trees became a thousand hungry claws reaching out to grab him. Standing before the slowly rocking figure – who was her lover and did she have children and dreams of some day leaving the village? – he would have strangled a child if the child was found guilty for the hanging. Anderson stood back and closed his eyes. "*The time is destitute,*" he thought, once again recalling a passage from his mini-thesis on Heidegger. "*It lacks the unconcealedness of the nature of pain and death and love. And this destitution is itself destitute because that realm of being withdraws within which pain and death and love belong together. But the song still remains which names the land over which it sings. What is the song itself? How is a mortal capable of it? Whence does it sing? How far does it reach into the abyss?*" He never knew what these words meant, but somehow he sensed that the very solution to their riddle, the deep hidden meaning behind the passage, was standing right in front of him. In a fit of rage he collapsed into a crouched position, pounding with his fists the earth before him as he cried out at the village, standing there in its gruesome silence, even the tertiary and quaternary echoes from his voice ringing out more loudly than the sound of a flock of cawing birds overhead.

I hate you Yugoslavia! I detest everything you are. You, the supposed cradle of Orthodox Christianity. You and your tall blonde soldiers and your Cyrillic script; you and your domed churches and promise of peace; you and your ethnic cleansing and your cities of plaster and stone; you and everything you've done to Mankind! Anderson looked up at the sky and followed the course of a circling hawk as it eyed an object of prey in final preparation before lunging into a dive. His voice had now softened to a slow monotonic muttering as the words flowed out like a man in a state of exalted prayer. *Why did I persist with you when all you brought me was death? Now without Anna, now even without myself, I trudge through your fields and hills in search of resolution but all I encounter is more death and emptiness. You tore away my wife as you tear away everything inside you and around you. You vanish when I reach out to grasp your essence, but when I turn away you strike back with the force of a thunderbolt. I came searching for fulfillment but I leave you as though running from an empty palace, with only the echoes of death to fill your crumbling halls.*

He let his head sink to the ground. Cradled in a small lump in the grass, he slowly opened his ears to the world around him. The wind hissed through the grass, the subtle crescendos and silences almost seeming to form the opening phrases of some brooding symphony. In counterpoint to the grass was the deeper and richer sound of leaves rustling on a nearby tree, creating a separate musical voice that was at once distinct but also somehow woven into the undulations of the grass. He stood up and gazed directly ahead of him; the woman continued to swing gently back and forth as if to say that his outcries had been meaningless and the world was mute to all forms of justice and retribution. Was he not for that instant the man from the ancient proverb who *in seeking revenge was forced to dig two graves*? In leaving Anna had he not subjected both of them to something much worse than either of them could ever had imagined?

He made his way out of the village down a clay road that eventually narrowed to a path funneling into a dense wooded area. The trees were rich with yellow-brown leaves that were burnished with tiny flakes of gold in the clear light of the sun. Still holding the gun that he had pried from the hands of the dead man, he stopped at a small stone bridge that arched up as though the two opposing banks had once been further apart and in narrowing the passage of the river had forced the bridge to pucker upwards. He set his first foot onto the wooden planks of the bridge and then withdrew it. The dead woman hanging in the churchyard had changed everything. He dug the heels of his shoes into the earth beneath him. It was only that morning he felt liberated and free, painting a portrait of his future like an artist before a blank canvas, but as he stood there in total silence a new and potentially much darker thought began to trouble him. What if Anna was in danger? Whoever was responsible for the killings could just as well kill her if she was ever so unlucky as to cross paths with them. As he set his foot back on the bridge he felt small and worthless, the sort of man he would have previously condemned. Even if she drove him to abandon her, pushing things so far that he could have only viewed himself as a fool for staying and putting up with it, it might still have been wrong to leave her. But if she really did run off with the solider and deceive him *yet again*, what measure of punishment, if any, was just, and if she was guilty did he have the right to decide what sentence she deserved and who should give it to her?

Two large thunderclouds gathered on the horizon like a pair of great hands preparing to lay waste to the earth. The air was filled with a scent like rainwater and minerals, filling his lungs with an energy he had not felt since arriving at the village. On the north bank of the river was a rim of white gravel stretching out about six yards from the water for as far as he could see in either direction. There were small twigs and creases in the otherwise smooth area, giving the impression of writing of some kind scribbled on a wall in the back alley of a train station. Whatever the signs or words meant – if anything at all – they became the expression of a great terrestrial history as though the entire world was part of a vast library and each thing, every last branch and every last being or breath drawn in or exhaled was a book, a chapter, a paragraph, or even a sentence in this vast lexicon of existence. Yet this only leant a sense of randomness to the world at large, rather than one of predestination – as the collection of events was so large that what happened in his life, whatever road, path, or sequence of bifurcations that he crossed was ultimately a function of which book he chose to open and become involved in rather than that particular book governing his experiences. A man in a library can never hope to read all the books at his disposal and those books he chooses and in which sequence he reads them and what reflections he has while reading them make up the substance of his day.

There was a clap of thunder and the air was filled with the sound of falling rain although he did not see any rain at first. However much he wished he could turn the clock back and change things, whatever was going to happen to him and whatever had already happened to Anna or might yet happen to her was completely out of his hands. She could be dead or she could be alive. If dead he would never see her again, yet if she was alive he might not ever get back together with her. That all depended on how he felt and how she felt and if either of them cared enough to make things work: all factors that seemed utterly beyond his control. How would he feel about her the next time he saw her, if he indeed ever saw her again? It was a question he had no way of answering. She could be the dazzlingly voluptuous heir of some metaphoric Grande Europa – the very woman she was in his imagination when he first met her and opened his soul to her in all its pettiness and beauty - or she could be that cheap tart that dumped him for a romp in the bushes with a soldier. But did she even run off with the solider and was he too hasty in coming to this conclusion in the first place? For a moment everything became random, as though the moral universe was flying on a renegade pathway through space and time and how he felt or why he felt was so far out of his reach that he might just as well be a limitless and solitary void – both empty and almighty in its blank white dominion.

III

The sky was layered with ribbons of clouds, almost unearthly in the intensity of their blue-gray hues, when Anderson emerged from a thinly forested area and entered a large open field. The horizon stood in clear view between two small mountain ridges and at the base of the northernmost mountain he could make out a small wooden chateau or summer cottage. As he neared the weatherworn rustic structure, the slender form of a man materialized out of the green and yellow backdrop of straw and grass stretching outwards from the base of the slope. As the man got closer he assumed the qualities of an abstract concept, a Janus-faced notion of threat and danger, novelty and becoming. This was the first person he met since leaving Anna, and the very act of greeting him was a task Anderson wasn't sure he was ready to face. He clutched the handle of the dead man's gun, which he had been keeping safely hidden in his pocket, and righted his posture. What would anybody be doing living alone in such a place? Was the man in need of help? Was he hiding from something or someone? Had he seen the massacre and, if he had, was he in any way involved?

When the figure was thirty yards away, Anderson loosened his grip on the gun and let it slip down to the base of his pocket and waved his hand in a gesture of surrender. The man, who looked too old and withered to be dangerous, raised his gaze from the ground and waved back in a way that was neither official nor casual. Anderson accelerated into a light jog, holding his hands high in the air to let the man know he was approaching in peace and had nothing to hide.

"English," Anderson cried.

"Hello," the man shouted back in a thick Croatian accent. From his short beard and round glasses alone he looked like a person who had spent many long years in a library or monastery, but his soiled jeans and bright red nylon racing jacket told a different story, his life seeming to embody the accidental confluence of two entirely different patterns of human existence. He walked with a cane in his right hand, and his arms moved with a different cadence than his legs, suggesting that the cane was not for any disability but some kind of prop or possibly a weapon used in self-defense.

"I'm lost," Anderson said in a way that was neither threatening nor disarming, minding the subtle balance between caution and trust that was developing.

"You look as though you could use a bath and a good meal," the man replied. He had a strange look of recognition in his eyes as though he had secretly been tracing Anderson's progress since leaving Pozega. "Where are you from?"

"I'm American...a journalist."

"You're not the first person that came running through these hills over the last few days."

Anderson let his arms drop to his side slowly, so as not to put the man on guard. There was a sudden rush of wind between them. "Were there other Americans?" Anderson asked.

"There was a soldier just yesterday. He was alone and said he had deserted and needed help. I gave him directions to a village over the mountain." He pointed his hand backwards without looking.

"What did he look like?" Anderson asked with acute interest.

"He was young and blonde, that's all I remember."

"Did he say anything about a girl?" Anderson clenched his hands together nervously and moved his palms around in a circular motion like a person trying to keep warm. "I don't recall if he did. But I usually remember everything, so he probably didn't."

"What was he wearing?"

The man paused as though he was struggling to add up a long sequence of figures in his head. Had he seen more? Was he just lying to cover up what he knew about Anna? "Street clothes and an olive drab army helmet."

Anderson paused in thought. Although the description suggested the two men were different, it was possible the soldier had just left Anna behind and had managed to steal a new set of clothes somewhere along the way. It was also possible they were following the same path northwards that Anderson had, since going back to Pozega would have meant facing the advancing troops and moving East would have meant walking into the jaws of the prisoner of war camps.

"Are you sure there wasn't a girl?" Anderson squinted his eyes the way of a teacher probing for an answer from a stubborn student.

There was a long silence and a second gust of wind blew between them. Anderson studied the man's face with its deep furrowed brow and long, almost goat-like chin. There was a strange look of displacement about him as though he didn't fit into any particular time or place. With his gentle but imposing demeanor, he reminded Anderson of a man he once knew named Jed Parsons. Parsons was a lonely but once very popular man who had never seemed in touch with whatever external prompting or innate wisdom usually flags a person to what is expected of him at any given stage of life. One day it dawned on him that he was forty, unmarried, and had never considered a long-term career. His friends – longtime drinking buddies - had all moved onto other things and now had lives that didn't remotely resemble his own. Over the next few months he started showing up uninvited to married couple dinner parties where he would try to show off whatever knowledge he had of current events as if to impress people enough to get him invited the next time. "It's time to invest in stocks, " he would say out of the blue without any detailed knowledge of the stock market when everyone knew it was a transparent attempt to make it look like he was keeping abreast of modern developments in the business world. "One can't get enough vitamins," he once declared as he bit into what everyone guessed was his first vegetable in over a month. "We all know how important health is to leading a successful life." A year later the man stopped showing up the soirees and a few months later someone Anderson knew received an invitation to Parson's funeral. Anderson never found out how Parsons died, but everyone suspected it was suicide. "What else could he have done?" Anna once asked in the tone of assertion one morning while she was vigorously beating a bowl of eggs with a fork. "You guys would have just gone on mocking him forever if it hadn't happened. Now you can ennoble yourselves by feeling sorry for him." Anderson was angry at her insinuation but knew in some morose way that she was right.

"Would you like to come to my house for some food and drink?" the Croat finally said, ignoring Anderson's last question. "You look like you could use a rest."

Anderson nodded his head with deliberate conviviality and the two walked together down the hill past a small patch of short grass, clumps of slender white mushrooms randomly popping out of the earth like tiny fragments of driftwood from a sand bar. Anderson told the man about the village and the dead men he had seen and the woman hanging from the rope and how he had seen the sign of an eagle and wondered if it was a paramilitary organization or just some battalion under strict orders to exterminate the inhabitants of certain villages. The man's eyes were filled with numbed regret rather than outrage as he explained that he knew nothing of the event but that such occurrences were tragically becoming more common since the war had started.

"I left law school in Vienna years ago to live a life of stoicism in the quiet of the mountains. I wanted to embrace all of God's creatures and step away from the world that man had created for himself. I came here to cultivate a peace of the soul and spirit. I spent hours walking along the tiny paths that the small rivers of rainwater had carved out for me. I read Aurelius. I tended my garden. I shunned all contact with the outer world."

Anderson walked beside in silence, noticing the disturbing way the man kept looking down at Anderson's legs as though he were following the progress of a small but deadly spider. They entered the small wooden house where there was the musty smell of mold and cool humidity. The kitchen was sparsely furnished with a simple pine table surrounded by a set of wooden crate-like chairs. The only light in the room cast thick golden rings on the walls and ceiling from inside a small oil lamp. The man walked in slow, almost pained steps, like those of a musician who has run dry of all emotions, having devoutly poured his life's every feeling into his work, into the kitchen. Less than a minute later he came back with a brown bag and set it on the table. Wasn't it odd that he had not yet introduced himself? It seemed he was following some kind of religious formality that necessitated suppression of any individual personality traits. In the present case, the embodiment of this ritual was the cutting of bread and meat and the laying out of fruits in a shallow porcelain bowl on the table.

"Why don't you sit down," the man said. Anderson thanked him and sat down.

As they ate the room became darker and the man's face slowly changed, becoming harder and more fixed in texture. It was as though his true self had emerged from beneath layers of masquerade and in this gradual unconcealing an enormous silence had opened up inside him, reaching outwards to engulf the room and everything in it. They faced each other like pure beings of the sky, earth, and water, divorced entirely from societal needs.

"Why have you come?" he finally said as though forced him into speech by the coming darkness. "Why have you of all people ended up sitting in that very chair across from me at this time when you could just as well have ended up lying dead on a battlefield or walking happily down the sidewalk to your house? Why did you disturb my solitude? Why did you not stay in the comfort of satellite dishes, baby carriages, loosely hung laundry, and old milk cartons piled up on the edges of deserted alleyways?"

Anderson clutched his gun as he studied the man's dark marble eyes. He bit into a stick of goose sausage and the smell in the room suddenly became more precise and therefore more stifling. It was the smell of the restaurant, located in a stone basement room in Paris, where he had once had dinner with Anna. They had sat in their wooden chairs like monks in an abbey squinting only slightly at the gray luminous light that poured in from the street through the small barred and oblong openings just below the point where the walls met the ceiling. Glasses clinked with shimmering opulence and occasionally the room would shudder with the sound of a train passing somewhere in the distance while they ate their dinner and sipped ruby-colored wine from their glasses – a bottle of 1964 *Richebourg*, a wine that Anderson would always come to associate with Anna and how she had looked that day as she sat across the table from him. A sense of unbridled excess, the pulchritudinous cheeks of young royalty in gowns and soft white skin distilled and concentrated through generations of enraptured aristocracy and a close attachment to the rituals of the earth and the fervent sensuality of starlit evenings, filled his being. Anna and the taste of the wine became one. She was wearing a tight white top, intricate knitted patterns and lace running in tight arabesques up and down her thin, and supple arms. Her straw colored hair – he was only later to find out that her natural color was darker – fell to her shoulders and across her face as she smiled with the innocence of a child stepping in from the rain. Captivated by the unearthly glow of her eyes he had watched the candle light dance off the wine glasses and her face as she played with the tiny ties and rivulets of her hair. The wine spread its phantom fingers across the table, intertwining broken rays of deep orange light from the candles in the room with strands of her yellow hair and scents of juniper, wet stones, saddle leather, and Asian duck.

Anderson tightened his jaws, grinding his teeth together so loudly he was sure the man would take it as a threat and ask him to leave. The same tender creature, who had stared so deeply into his soul so many countless times that summer and well before, was possibly dead. Across the table the man continued to chew on a piece of bread that he had been struggling with for almost a minute. With every breath of the suffocating musk-like odor in the room his sense of loss intensified until finally Anderson could take no more. He stood up abruptly and cleared his throat.

"I need to get to the nearest village," he said. His hands were now trembling. "I have to find that soldier."

The man seemed to understand Anderson's request before he had finished the sentence. He nodded his head in solemn acknowledgement and then left the room. A minute later he came back with a second oil lamp and a piece of paper. He lit the lamp and turned it higher to its brightest setting and then began to draw a row of what looked like geometrical figures on the paper.

"Virovitica is not so far," he said. "You first have to pass across a small range of mountains." He pressed his pencil down on the piece of paper and continued drawing. "You are here," he said, pointing to a house he had just drawn below a rise of V-shaped figures Anderson took to be the mountains. Then he drew a small city on the far side of the furthest mountain and then he drew a line from that village – represented by a collection of steeples bunched closely together – back through the mountains, weaving in long and alternating arcs to the other side.

"First you must walk along to a river to the north." He pointed towards one of the walls in the room. "Then you must follow the direction of the sun's motion along the river until you get to the city. It should only take you a day. Then you can ask around." The man suddenly looked doubtful as he dropped the pencil to the table and then folded the map and handed it to Anderson. "You might also want to take the rest of the bread."

Anderson reached out for the bread and nodded his head in gratitude. Then he stood up as though to signal the end of their interchange. He gathered his things together and walked to the door. His eyes stopped on a small red gyroscope that he had previously failed to notice. He wondered if it had once belonged to a child, and if so, was that child still alive somewhere – maybe hidden away in the depths of the house. It was an evil thought, the kind of thought he was embarrassed to have allowed enter his head.

But didn't the man have a strangely unsettling aura emanating from beneath his calm and composed countenance? The man followed behind.

"The mountains have a way of hiding things and then revealing them again when you least expect it. I've lived here for ten years and have had the fortunate – or unfortunate - luxury of having too much time on my hands. In the evenings I've been able to study the patterns of the mountains' every twitch and shadow. The clouds, the wind, the rain, the trees. They all have their own language. But when you find what you want you may realize it wasn't what you originally wanted or you no longer want it. That's why I moved away from the city." The man paused and looked down at the gyroscope. Anderson wondered what he was thinking. The man took a deep breath and continued. "Apartment life. My cat staring blankly out the window into a night I could no longer understand or even begin to grasp. Life takes you away from things you once loved and forces new things on you until you no longer know what it was you wished for and why you desire whatever it is you now crave for."

Anderson shook the man's hand to thank him and acknowledge that his words had touched him – although he wasn't sure they had - and walked outside. When he heard the heavy wooden door shut behind him he knew it was the beginning of another quest, and a feeling came over him that what would happen in the end was completely beyond his control or comprehension. If the man was right and the mountains were really protecting Anna as she hid away in silence, then the moment the massive stone deities decided to free her and bring her back to him was also out of his control. But believing this line of thought was tantamount to fatalism, so all he could do was hope this wasn't true and that his efforts to find her would have a tiny effect and somehow change things in some hidden or direct way as to tilt things in his favor and bring Anna back to him.

Anderson let his hands drop to his side and began to walk in blank and precise steps in the direction dictated by the man. He looked upwards. The sky held out what seemed like an offering of clouds for an imminent ritual of nature. He had never seen such a thick profusion of shapes and textures. In one corner of the sky hovered wide and flat clouds with tight grill-like markings giving the impression of a giant automobile radiator moving aimlessly towards the horizon. In the south, directly above a gathering of dark Cypresses, sailed a collection of small, truffle-like clouds hemmed by light wispy edges and smooth rounded bottoms that tapered upwards into twisted points. And on the opposite horizon he could see a wash of dark gray thunderclouds spreading like thick pools of blood across the sky - a portent of impending danger. In the west there were long streaks of barely perceptible white clouds, occupying spaces much higher in elevation than the others. These clouds were almost heavenly in their frailty and balanced out the more threatening nature of the darker formations to the north.

The horizon, the landscape, and everything else around him took on the proportions of a metaphor for life and how you always had a choice of doing one thing or another thing and did what you always thought was best even though later it didn't turn out to be that way. There were threatening forces that you shied away from or outright avoided for self-preservation, and nurturing or enriching forces that you drew in or followed because you felt it was the only source of beauty in your otherwise barren existence. But sometimes, as in the case of the soldier and how Anderson left him with Anna, walking away to redeem your pride was not the best thing to do, although you never had a way of knowing this except in retrospect. Similarly, you never knew whether it was wise to always walk away from danger – as a man who always runs for cover when the sky turns dark green and a funnel cloud appears and begins to stretch downwards – or instead summon all courage and face the threat and try to eliminate it even though you think it may be far too dangerous and you never could anyway?

Anderson adjusted the buttons of his shirt as he observed a small grouping of trees rocking back and forth in the wind. Whatever he believed, the whole situation would never have happened if he hadn't married Anna in the first place and brought her to Yugoslavia. Thus, while his marriage initially seemed good and pure, it ultimately led to something far more questionable and now treacherous. Marrying her to find solace in his life was thus like avoiding a coming storm by walking in the direction of the whiter clouds and blue sky only to find they led to a much greater danger than he could ever have imagined and that he would have been better off not marrying and staying put to weather the passing of the thunderclouds instead.

He walked for what seemed like almost an hour before he turned around and noticed that he could still see the house in the background. He felt demoralized by his lack of progress. The world suddenly became a giant treadmill, with every step forward really just one step backward. Every insight or connection created one more level of confusion he was forced to deal with that would ultimately draw him even further away from whatever it was he thought his goal was. As he continued walking, in strict but distant parallel to a narrow road passing in smooth curves over a gentle slope, on top of which stood a stone mill and a well, before falling again down another slope into a shallow valley which, from the distance took on the form of a vast ocean of blood, so intensely red were the flowers that matted its base. If the man was indeed telling the truth, it would not be long before Anderson was in Virovitica.

IV

Anderson edged along the white clay and gravel path that lined the riverbank, carefully stepping over wet clumps of grass and soil, and then over and beyond long sandy patches prickly with sharp twigs and rocks alike. Everything was exactly as the man had described. The village slowly came into view behind a gate of deep green poplars; to his left stood a natural gallery formed by a circle of large rectangular boulders. It was almost night. A warm breeze wafted from the direction of the village as he focused his gaze on a tall slender spire rising from the center of a light blue onion dome a few hundred meters away. The village would soon be his judge and once it had passed its verdict he might know what had happened to Anna. Every leaf and blade of grass, every grain of sand and every bird or insect would conspire to form his jury. His crime was one of doubt and retaliation crystallized by the petty and barbarous act of leaving Anna in the hands of a complete and utter stranger in times of war. Because of this he was no longer worthy of her love and deserved to meet whatever fate had befallen her. If he was lucky the village would show its forgiveness and she would be there, safe and whole, waiting to take him into her arms. Only then would he be granted a pardon and be allowed to be with her again. Yet did he even deserve its forgiveness?

He passed a wooden house on the edge of the riverbank, which rose up gently behind the back of the house to finally merge with a small cliff, layered with gradations of alternating red and cream colored stone. A small black-haired child was sitting on a patch of sand reading a book and whistling in a sad purposeful way. He wondered if that same child had crossed paths with Anna and if so what impressions she had made on him. Would the child have regarded her as the image of a potential savior or merely an indifferent foreigner? Or would she have made no impression at all on the boy? Anderson continued along the riverbank and up the slope towards the cliff, on the other side of which stood a row of brick townhouses beside a tall black cistern.

The center of the town was larger than the entire previous village in which the massacre had occurred. The streets were lined with urns stuffed with brightly colored flowers and these urns were alternated down the blocks with tall Gothic lamps constructed from hanging glass bulbs encased in elegant wrought iron loops. As he made his way through a series of crooked side streets, he was suddenly overcome by the impression that he could just as well be walking through some northern European city like Bruges or Hamburg. There was definitely something Hansian about the architecture. The roads were constructed from pieces of large rounded cobblestone and the cracks between the each stone were thick and green with soft velvety moss. He also noticed that the sun was casting longer shadows than just a day before, as though it was suddenly several months later and autumn was at its end. This made him feel calm and secure, closer to himself than the outside world, a sensation that often came over him as winter approached and the hustle and bustle of summer had finally died down.

He stopped at a post office and steppeded inside. A woman with a long stolid face, red hair, and a large gold necklace that looked too expensive for somebody in her place, was sitting behind the counter. She looked at him as he approached her but her expression didn't change.

"I'm looking for a soldier," he said. "Or rather a woman."

The woman looked at him before looking quickly away as though busied with something of greater importance.

"They would have passed through yesterday or today. The woman was American. They may or may not have been together."

Anderson waited for a reply. She raised her eyebrow in acknowledgement of his statement, although her face still did not alter in any way its original appearance.

"You have to help me," he pleaded. "There was a massacre in a small village near here."

She nodded her head in acknowledgement. "Some say a soldier did it and then ran away to hide from the police," she said, suddenly more interested and helpful, as though whatever preoccupation that had kept her from expressing herself was revealed as show and nothing more.

"What did this soldier look like?" Anderson asked desperately.

"Are you with the army?"

"No," he said. There was a smell liked burned beef in the room that he hadn't noticed before. "But I'm family. I need to find the girl."

"He wasn't with a woman," she said pointedly. Anderson relaxed inside. His shoulders felt more loose and pliant. She was safe or it was a different man. But then a darker thought flew through his mind. Maybe he had already killed her before he crossed the village. "Who told you to come?"

"A man who lives on the other side of the mountain in a small house." Anderson pointed back in the direction from which he had come. "He told me someone in this village could help me."

She leaned toward the glass that was separating them as though to pass on a secret. "I think you are best staying out of this. A lot of people go missing and those who ask questions often go missing as well. You have to let those with power get their way or they might end up getting their way with you as well."

It was an attitude that always surprised him no matter how often he had encountered it here, one that permitted any amount of injustice in exchange for whatever seemed the easiest and safest path for everyone.

"Who can I talk to?" he asked, ignoring her warning.

"Go to the restaurant by the boat house," she said portentously. "An old woman there keeps tabs on everything. She might help you if you make it worth her while."

She told him how to get there and then he thanked her and walked out of her post office and down a narrow path between two stone fences towards a small diamond-shaped park. From the other side of the park extended what appeared to be a street – if the woman had indeed given him good directions – which, if he followed it to the end, would take him to the said boathouse. At the end of the path an olive-colored lizard darted in front of him before stopping to inspect him, and then raced away, disappearing under a large stone just a few feet away.

He walked through the park, passing a bench where a man sat reading a newspaper. A dog lay beside him in silent obedience. As Anderson approached, the dog began to wag its tail earnestly. But when Anderson stopped and extended his hand to pat it on the head, the dog seemed suddenly frightened and so looked over towards its owner, who hadn't seemed to notice that anybody else was in the park, and then looked back at Anderson with a look of growing desperation in its eyes as though it were waiting for some higher orders, or at least some kind of reassurance, it now knew would never come. He stepped back and the dog suddenly jumped out at him, freezing in mid air for a moment as it reached the end of its chain half way through its leap and then bolting back with a quick jerk. The man looked up from his paper and pulled the chain lightly as if to call the dog back to his side.

"You should keep an eye on your dog," Anderson shouted over his shoulder as he walked away. The dog started barking wildly, stretching the chain to its limit, but the man had retreated once again behind his newspaper, apparently too wrapped up in whatever he was reading to take much notice.

Anderson walked until he found a road that he guessed was the same one the woman had told him to follow and then turned in the same way she had directed him. The road was lined with a row of red and blue diesel trucks with the word "Lux" printed in bright yellow letters on the side. As though controlled by an invisible switchboard, a dark blue bird flew over the roof of the first truck at the same time a jet of gray smoke bellowed upwards from its tall silver exhaust pipe. Down the street a siren wailed for a moment as though to acknowledge the event.

The boathouse was two blocks further down. It was surrounded on three sides by stately majestic pine trees and on the fourth by the river. The dock was empty and still, leaving the impression of an abandoned parking lot atop the wind-rippling but otherwise still waters of the river. From a distance the square structure - seemingly built more out of service to function than aesthetics - appeared to be made of wood, but as he got closer he could see that it was actually beige stucco coating the outer walls that only looked like wood. Next to it stood a small tavern-style restaurant with wrought iron lanterns fixed on either side of the large oak doors. In front of the boathouse and directly beside the riverbank a large woman wearing a bright blue dress sat on a bench that looked far too small for her gargantuan form. She looked old, but was she the person Anderson was looking for? She was leaning over and knitting a small sweater – perhaps for a baby – and was whistling just like the boy he had seen earlier. He wondered if it was the same morose tune the boy had whistled - he couldn't tell for sure – and if it was, what was the most likely link between the two people and what was the significance of the tune, if any? Perhaps it was a death march for a man everyone had hated and the entire town was glad to see once and for all the man buried in the ground. Or maybe the woman was related to the boy and the tune was in honor of a kind relative they both were mourning the loss of.

Anderson was just about to greet the woman but then he stopped. The first woman at the post office had told him to look for an old woman *in* the restaurant, and since this woman was not quite inside the restaurant, Anderson decided first to walk in and start his search inside rather than risk a potentially embarrassing conversation with the woman whistling in front of him. As he approached the restaurant he resolved to pretend he knew as little as possible. That was the safest. All he would reveal was that he was looking for a soldier who may or may not have been with an American woman the day he had possibly passed through.

He pushed open the doors of the restaurant and walked in. The dining area was dimly lit by a set of wall lanterns – much like the ones on either side of the outermost door – and there were four heavy wooden tables evenly spaced in a rectangular pattern occupying the center of the room. By the bar near the far wall three men were talking to a woman Anderson assumed was a waitress because of her dull eyes but forward and flirtatious manner. One of the men had deep-set eyes and an older, weatherworn face giving him the look of a retired sea captain. He kept pointing at a picture in a newspaper laying flat on top of the bar, beckoning for the waitress to come over and take a closer look. She posed insouciantly beside the other two men who were both light haired and younger than the first, each competing against the other to engage her in conversation. The two men were dressed in soiled work clothes and were both smoking, taking long, almost exhibitionist draws on their cigarettes that reminded Anderson of film clips he had seen in which chimpanzees were trained to smoke like French film stars. The woman's eyes darted back and forth as she attempted to keep both parties happy while committing herself completely to neither. No one seemed to notice as Anderson walked up to the bar and stopped directly behind the waitress.

"I'm looking for woman," he said. "American."

The three men continued talking to the waitress as if Anderson wasn't even in the room. He was so close behind her he could smell her hair, still fragrant with a recent shampooing. He moved his hand to tap her on the shoulder, but instead he just spoke.

"Excuse me," he said. "I'm looking for..."

The waitress swept around, her long black hair brushing against him. "No English," she said.

"A woman with a soldier," he said very slowly. He turned his eyes to the man with the newspaper, who was looking directly at Anderson in cold derision that belied his otherwise gentle appearance. Anderson lifted his eyebrows as though to repeat his question and the man shrugged his shoulders, signaling that he didn't speak English either. The waitress walked briskly away towards a door to what Anderson guessed was the kitchen.

"American woman," Anderson said to the two other men who had been watching him, thin smirks on their faces.

"*Stay away from me*," one of them sang out in broken English to the tune of the *Guess Who* song. Then he started twisting his arms and torso back and forth as if he were dancing in a discotheque.

"Do you speak English?" Anderson asked. The man stopped gyrating on his stool.

"No English," the two men said in unison. They broke out laughing and the man who had been singing started twisting his torso again.

Anderson walked back and sat down at a table. He had forgotten that he still had some money with him and also that he was hungry. He might as well eat something as he waited for someone to come in, maybe the fat woman outside, who could possibly help him. Perhaps she was the old woman he was looking for after all.

When the waitress came out from the kitchen, Anderson raised his hand in a gesture of readiness to order, but she just walked past him without acknowledgement and went back to standing with the three men. Anderson cleared his throat loudly and then coughed, hoping to get her attention. She turned around and looked harshly at him and then whispered something in the ear of the man who looked like a sea captain. The man turned to look at Anderson and then turned back to the waitress and nodded. Anderson guessed they had noticed something unusual and maybe even humorous about his appearance. Maybe there was something on his face and he hadn't noticed. He wiped his hand surreptitiously across his nose and then coughed. The waitress smiled and whispered something to the other two men. Anderson thought he heard something in English. It was just a small whisper, yet it was discernable nonetheless and maybe intentionally so. "Doesn't he just look ridiculous sitting there like he owns the place?"

"What?" Anderson asked loudly, reminding himself that he still had a gun in his pocket.

"*American woman,*" the man cried out again as he looked over at Anderson. "*Stay away from mee-eee!*"

"I'd like something to eat," Anderson asserted himself. The waitress was now emptying an ashtray into a small plastic bag. She looked up at him and shrugged her shoulders. The three men burst out laughing.

Anderson froze his expression and locked glances with her. Around her wrist was wrapped a pink plastic band with a large white Mickey Mouse watch attached at the center. What right did they have to just stand there and mock him? From what pulpit of superiority were they grinning and leering at him? Who had granted them the divine privilege to stand in judgment over him? Wasn't this effrontery born from exactly the same attitude that led to the woman being hung from the tree in the small village? The four of them were enemies of Anna and hence the rest of humanity. He stood up sharply and walked over to the bar. By the time he had crossed the room their thin taunting grins had flattened and their gazes were less resolute.

"Where the hell is she?" Anderson said. He grabbed the sea captain by the shirt collar and stared fiercely into his frightened blue eyes. The waitress stepped back and picked up a sponge that had been sitting behind one of the beer taps. She started wiping the bar in short choppy strokes as the two other men looked down at their feet, pretending not to notice. "And don't pretend you don't know who I'm talking about."

"Ask the woman outside by the door," the man replied. His hands were shaking and he was breathing quickly. "She was working when the soldier came through."

Anderson let the man go and turned to walk out the door without saying a word. Silence was the best weapon. He pushed the door open without looking back and walked out into the light as he imagined Orpheus might have done when he left the underworld behind him, Eurydice calling out after him. Only this time he would not turn back.

The fat woman was still outside. From up close she looked as though she may once have been beautiful. Her cheeks were rounded yet still well defined and she had a yielding, but still composed and intelligent look that Anderson had always found attractive in women. He suppressed his anger as best he could as he found the words for speech.

"I hope I'm not disturbing you," he said. She turned to him with a look that invited him to say more, yet revealed nothing of what she might have thought of him.

"I'm looking for a woman," he said.

"American?" the woman asked in surprisingly clear English.

"Yes," he said. "We were separated by a storm in the hills and we never found each other again."

"Alone?"

"No. Or maybe she was. What I mean is that she may have been with somebody."

"There was a soldier here," she said sharply. She knew more and was obviously testing him to see how much he knew. "If you had anything to do with him then maybe you should leave."

"A soldier?" Anderson asked. "I was with my wife and we met a soldier and then I lost them. When I got to town I heard a soldier had just passed through here."

"A lot of soldiers come through. But he was different. There was something hard and cold in his eyes. In most of them you can see a person who was once a boy as they scream out their last words. But when he screamed it was somehow different."

"Different?" Anderson asked. He wondered what she meant by *last words*.

"You can check through his belongings," she said. "He left some of his clothes by the river before he left. Must have forgotten them. Better I turn around and sell them, than they do." She pointed to the door of the restaurant.

She went into the boathouse and came back with a sack. She pulled it open and carefully removed each item as though she were preparing to display them at a market. The shirt was the same one the soldier was wearing the day Anderson had abandoned them and the shoes were also the same. There was no sign of anything belonging to Anna.

"Do you know where he was sleeping before he came?" he asked.

"He said he was staying in an abandoned church up the side of that mountain." She pointed to a jagged white peak in the distance. "But I guess he could have been lying," she laughed. "He looked like a liar."

Convinced that he had heard enough, he thanked the woman and walked quickly back along the road towards the park where he had earlier seen the man and his dog. When he got there the man was gone, a small lizard having taken his place in clear view on the bench as though protecting its nest. He wondered if it was the same lizard he had seen before. If it was, maybe it was a sign that he was lucky and that he might also find Anna. He took a deep breath and accelerated into a jog as he retraced his path down the narrow trail, past the post office, and finally outside of town in the direction of the mountain peak.

His legs began to tire and he slowed to a light jog, a dark feeling gradually coming over him that he was just a fool for thinking there was any hope. From the solitary man who had guided him to the village to the various women who had led him to where he was now going it all seemed too pat, and because of this something had to be wrong. There was no reason to trust the woman by the boathouse – perhaps she had just discovered those clothes in some alleyway and wanted to sell them - and so there might be nothing at all on the mountain peak and even if there was the soldier could still be a different man than the one he was looking for, possibly even the same one who had committed the massacre in the village. As he made further beyond the outskirts of the city, he passed a small hut constructed from dried twigs that somehow spoke of destitution and loss. He turned his gaze upwards. The sky had assumed the same nondescript blue-gray color of the hundreds of state-built apartment complexes he had once passed and photographed on the outer rim of Budapest. It was at that moment that he felt the deepest pain in all his life, a feeling he would never forget until the day he died.

V

As Anderson walked up the mountainside the sun began to set and with it the daylight slowly waned. Tall shadows wavered in the trees and bushes like a hundred tiny sylphs dancing and lunging in the dying light as they waited for further darknesses to spring up like black fountains from the earth and spread outwards into the world. A chemical scent like shoe polish or petroleum filled the air. Had the soldier been somewhere nearby? Anderson passed through a filed of heather and then small grove of trees, their drooping branches dressed with thick green leaves that seemed to glow and reflect a pallid unnatural light. The ground was muddy and several times he slipped. Every time he reached what he thought was the summit of the mountain, he discovered that it was only a small plateau, a step on the way up to a much higher peak that was hidden somewhere beyond the horizon of his vision, meted out by the dense green walls of fir trees that lined the mountainside. At one point he lost his breath and had to stop beside a natural gully to gather his strength. He reassured himself that it could not be that much further before he reached the peak, since from the base it had not appeared to be a particularly tall mountain.

After some time he came upon a barren glacial valley dotted with tiny piles of gravel. The cairns were arranged in a loose circle roughly one hundred meters across, giving the impression that they had been left there as sign posts for some navigational or religious purpose. Here and there were piled waist-high heaps of melting snow, since gone gray and brown from the dust and wind. At the end of this clearing the land dipped downwards and then tilted upwards again as if taking a break before preparing for its final ascent. He followed a ridge of ice until he was at the base of the small valley and then he stopped to take another rest. Perhaps

Anna had stood on that very spot screaming for help as the soldier towered over her to ravage her weak and defenseless form.

He stopped as the sun sank beneath a bed of clouds on the great western horizon. In the fading light of dusk, the world became a vast profusion of reckless forms tearing away into the very emptiness that defined them. First there was nothingness, and then like crystals growing in a jar these forms blossomed forth into their existence. A light wind blew through his hair and he felt a cold shudder, reminding him that he was alone and vulnerable and in need of shelter. He turned a full three hundred and sixty degrees before stopping and resting his gaze on the figures of nature that stood before him. There, a bush with its sharp stabbing leaves and tightly-wound red flowers that smelled like pencil lead or sage brush, and beside it a jutting stone flat and honed to a serried edge that stretched out into the air. He thought he could smell something like juniper berries and rotting flesh as he set one foot forward to start once more his quest. As soon as his other foot followed he was suddenly possessed by the feeling of being "one who is in motion" as opposed to "one who is wandering" or even worse, "one who is idle and always will be" and with this feeling he sprang into a run and propelled himself through a field of waist-high duckweeds and bramble bushes until he reached a jagged stone crest on the other side of which stood a small shack. He stopped for a moment and then ran even faster in the direction of its dark red walls.

She would be inside, he thought. And all would be well. He was just being overly protective to think that harm had come to her in any way. Feelings had always guided him to the truth in the past. Whenever he had experienced a premonition about a coming event or turn in a relationship, he was usually right. And those times he felt lucky, a man to whom fortune would bow any minute, something good had always happened: he would find a coin on the road or make a new acquaintance that would later help him in some critical way. Perhaps it was the expression of some greater psychological law that scientists would one day grab hold of and formulate into a physics of the mind and ether. Time ran on like a river and like a river it had its eddies and back flows from which could be read the tiny inflections that signaled changes in the current up or downstream.

Beads of sweat dripped from his forehead, becoming cold even before they fell away from his brow, as he neared the shack. He detected the smell of urine, suggesting that someone had recently been there. The door was closed, and the windows were shuttered, giving the hut the look of a clandestine meeting place where subversive plans were laid out in total silence with only the howling wind to bear witness. He clutched the brass doorknob and turned it. Then he pulled the door open without a trace of resistance from inside. He stepped across the threshold. Instead of the bare and rudimentary pigsty his imagination had conjured he found a quaintly furnished living room in the center of which stood an old blue couch and a coffee table beside it. By the door, a pair of slippers had been arranged in perfect order perpendicular to the wall, and beside these a worn bamboo cane was balanced against a higher patch of the same wall. There was no sign of anybody.

Being careful not to make too much noise, he walked into the middle of the living area and looked around. The room had the appearance of a scene in day-to-day life frozen in time as if someone had suddenly vanished without a disturbance after having lived there for years. The words "ice" and "age" hung heavily in his mind; he fell under the impression that he was isolated in a time frame that was doomed to leave nothing but fossils and artifacts of lives long since ended to future generations. Not only was he surrounded by the ice of the mountains that had been laid down there by the elements eons before, but the room itself had a certain frozen austerity that one would normally associate with old age. A small wooden table occupied the corner of the room; a long forest green scarf was folded neatly in the middle. He picked it up. Although he had no recollection of Anna ever owning such a scarf, it carried the lingering odor of her perfume and he was immediately transported back to a day they both once lay together in a dark room he no longer remembered where with only the wet pulse of her presence and the smell of her skin and sebum of her hair and also more strongly and fragrant her perfume in a cloud hovering around him like the breath of an angel that would always protect him from whatever darkness the world could ever hold, and yet so strangely too this enveloping aura was also a darkness of its own and in its own and special way, but one of oblivion and warmth shielding him from all that was harmful and unwelcome and containing all things at once that he would ever crave and hope for in this life or any other he could or could not imagine. Anna, Anna, Anna. When he let the scarf fall from his hands back onto the table he was suddenly overcome by a feeling he was being watched.

"Anna!" he shouted without restraint. A sharp and bitter feeling ran through him and the world darkened rapidly but also as though in notches controlling the intensity of his wanting.

There was no answer.

He dug his hands into his pocket and pulled out his gun. "I'll shoot," he whispered into the dread silence as though to an invisible marauder. He paced back and forth through the living room a few times before leaving to check the kitchen. It was decorated in faded green wallpaper, insipid interlocking fruit patterns raised slightly from the background in cheap velveteen stubble. The window was open and the curtains fluttered in the delicate breeze, as if to foreshadow the coming of a visitor. After rounding the house in the same repeated circuit for fifteen minutes without event, he stopped and picked up a small wooden box the size of a fist that was lying on the floor and opened its elegantly hinged lid. Inside was a piece of paper with a few numbers scribbled on it. He lifted the paper to his nose and inhaled, hoping to detect a trace of the perfume from the scarf. Nothing. It was almost odorless. He put the slip of paper back into the box and set it ceremoniously back on the floor.

He pulled a chair out from the corner and sat down, his gun firmly and solidly drawn like an ancient warrior guarding a secret tomb. If Anna had recently been here it was possible that she, with or without the soldier, would be back at any minute. After what seemed like several hours of silence, during which he wasn't sure he had fallen asleep for just a moment or not, he stood up. If they would not come to him, he had to go to them. If they had already left for good he had to search the area around the house for further clues. He stepped outside and closed the door behind him. The dawn light spilled across the horizon. It was clear from the scarf that Anna had been in the house and clear to his intuitions that she might even be somewhere in the vicinity that very moment, but to find her was going to take more stealth and effort. Behind the house were the remnants of a garden: browned and broken stalks of corn and a few morning glories climbing a short ornamental fence that seemed to have been erected out of caprice and not to shut out anything that lay beyond its borders. She must have gained some consolatory sense of peace while being here, he thought. It was soothing to imagine that even though she was the prisoner of the soldier she was held captive in this still and beautiful world, seemingly devoid of any outside disturbances.

There was a sharp pop in his ears and he suddenly became aware of the sound of gurgling water. He was far too high up the mountain for it to be a river, or even a brook, as the glacial run off always flowed downwards, carving paths in the rock as gravity pulled the water down to sea level. He focused his ears in the direction of the sound, but the noise had vanished as quickly as it came. Satisfied it was nothing important, he walked through the garden and beyond the perimeter of the small house. The ground was covered with black dirt the texture of dried blood and, apart from a few weeds pressing up from between a cluster of stones the size of a human head, there was no sign of growth until the bare dirt gave way to a thicket of low-cut bushes, each crowned by a layer of red-orange flowers blooming in perfect unison. When he fell into the range of the deep musky scent of the flowers he once again heard the sound of gurgling water, only this time more intensely. Certain it was coming from somewhere directly in front of him and beneath the thick layer of underbrush he knelt down, spreading two bushes apart with his hands to see if he could find the source. But instead of a lapping mountain spring there was only a shoelace shot through with dark black stains as though it had been used to tighten a tourniquet around a person's arm. He thrust his hand forward to pick it up but no sooner had he touched it with his fingers than he saw beneath it the tender white flesh of a woman's hand. He immediately recognized it by the slim gold wedding band and the long, elegantly bony fingers. *Transmit the preludes through his hair, so intimate that Chopin...*were the words that always rose inside him when she had caressed him in bed after practicing late into the night.

"Anna," he cried. He pulled at the arm but felt nothing but soft heavy weight that almost seemed to pull him back with an even greater force. He tore madly away at the underbrush, revealing her delicate body frame by frame as one might see a series of photos in a coroners office after a brutal murder. First the arm, slim and white, then the shoulder, bent and slightly crooked, yet gradually giving way to the smooth feminine contours of her neck and still lightly rouged face. When he pulled her out of the bushes and onto the wet earth she lay still on the black dirt, her clothes torn as with a knife. There were bloodstains on her cheeks. He shook her in sharp violent spasms, his shock and disbelief even more violent than his paroxysms. *Anna you can't. Anna, it's all my fault. Anna please come back and never speak to me again as I never deserved you. Anna I am so sorry for doubting you and even more for abandoning you. Anna, please just come back. Anna, Anna, Anna.* He stopped and felt her hand. It was cool but not yet cold. For a moment he imagined he heard the beating of a giant heart, but then it faded into the now rhythmical sound of the surging water, from where or even which direction he was still not sure.

He pulled her hand close to his cheek and inhaled. Her skin was soft and smelled like perfume and sweat. The scent of orange blossoms filled the air, folded in layers of other smells: decaying meat, saddle leather, licorice, and alpine flowers. His mind flashed back to the evening he had shared with her in the dank basement restaurant. Richebourg. It was a wine that he would always associate with death, as its name conjured up images of hemophiliacs and decadent royalty. But this time the smell was more real. There was a sudden breeze and the panoply of scents disappeared, replaced by an odor more like that of slate or gravel. He let her hand drop and pressed his cheek against hers. The skin was warm and silky to the touch. He could feel her eye lashes tickling his cheek as the soft wind blew gently through her hair. *Why did I leave you? Why did I abandon you in such selfishness? You always told me I would die the death of Diomedes falling into his own blade. You always said I was the needy one and without you I would fall to pieces. You always said you could do without me and only stayed with me because no one else but me would ever be so loyal. Now here I am again and you are dead as though to spite me one last time and prove me wrong. Prove that I ran away from you rather than coming back to save you. I hate you Anna. Despite all my love that knows no bound I still hate you. Like a God so sick of his own love of Man that he has learned to hate as the final expression of his everlasting Love...*

His soliloquy faded into the sound of a bird screeching in the distance. His inner dialogue lost momentum and slowed, finally becoming limp and veering away from its fatalistic path until it was no longer distinguishable from the random thoughts that tumbled through his mind like coded gibberish on a computer screen. Was it words that shaped and molded thoughts and ideas, or was it thoughts that were the blueprint and genesis of our every word? Was language *the house of being* as Heidegger had asserted, or was it the other way around? He lifted his head and stood up in grief. For the first time he noticed a pool of water near her body. He traced the large puddle with his eyes until it vanished in the underbrush. He took several steps forward and parted a tangling of branches in order to see further. Just as he was about to follow the pool deep into the bushes, in hope that he could find a spring that might supply him water pure enough to wash her delicate form, he heard something moving behind him. He stopped and turned around.

Anna was lying on the ground staring at him, one eye open and the other still closed, as though she were examining some exotic but frightful insect that had just landed on the branch in front of her.

"Anna," she said softly as though she recalled someone by that name but wasn't sure who it was or when she had even met such a person.

The sound of rushing water filled the air and he fell to his knees, letting the stiff sharp reeds rip through his pants as his knees pressed into the hard vegetal bed of the earth. He stood up slowly. Turning his head and almost stumbling over a root that protruded from its place in the ground so as to make the shape of an inverted bow, he spotted a second set of hands that were just visible still further back in the reeds and clasping a long wooden pole that stood erect and perpendicular to the ground. The hands were heavy and still, like those of a statue and gave way to a thick set of wrists emerging from an olive drab coat. Without saying anything Anderson lifted his pistol and pointed to a spot about three feet further back from the reeds and held it there for what seemed like an eternity until, under the shrill whisper of the wind, he heard a soft female voice from behind ask him to drop the gun.

He turned his head back and looked down at Anna, who was lying there on the ground staring at him with the large vacant eyes of one emerging from the depths of prayer. He knelt down beside her and dropped the gun, not once removing his gaze from her soft white face.

VI

Anderson lifted Anna from the ground as rain began to pour from the deep gray skies, now the color of asphalt. There was a sudden biting wind that seemed far too cold to sustain anything in liquid form, a grim reminder that summer was quickly losing foothold in the world. She staggered when he let go of her hand so he quickly slipped his arm behind her to brace her against a possible fall. There was a second rush of wind, but this time it was warm and damp as though bellowing from a hidden basement or the depths of some subterranean grotto, the opening conduit to which was somewhere close by.

"I'm so sorry," he said as he looked at her, fully understanding the futility of his words and how hollow they must have seemed to her. There was a clap of thunder and the rain yielded to a soft atomized form that now brushed lightly against his face.

"You're an asshole, Anderson," she said in a slow grinding whisper he had never heard from her before.

Anderson looked at her thoughtfully and then down at the ground. Anything he said – anything at all - would be taken as a crass attempt to clear himself of blame, and once he accepted blame she would think he had only done so superficially, in order to move on to some more facile emotional space between them and avoid facing the full gravity of his blamefulness.

"You left me with that creep. He could have killed me."

He lifted his hand to touch her forehead and wipe away the rain, but she drew away sharply, pushing it back as she shook her head back and forth in condemnation.

"You've lost the right to touch me," she said.

He looked at her pleadingly and then let this expression fade into one of shame and self-disgust.

"Are you hurt?"

"What does it matter? I could have been because of you and isn't that enough?"

"Anna, please...I thought you were cheating on me when I could not find you by the fire. I thought because you were allowing him to flirt with you that you were trying to start things up again. Life takes us away from things and distorts our true intentions," he said, mirroring what the hermit had told him.

"You're also full of shit. *Life takes us away*... How dare you try to dress this all up with some kind of cute maxim. It's so like you to romanticize your faults and try to turn them into some general expression of human folly."

He grabbed her hand and squeezed it even harder when she tried to pull away. "There is nothing I can say to absolve myself of blame, but I was sure you went off with him that night. What would you have done if I had just finished having an affair and then started flirting right under your nose with the first person that came along."

"You don't understand women very well," she said.

She started walking in heavy, self-conscious and deliberate steps back towards the shack. Anderson followed her, his eyes riveted in repulsion at the scene, the wooden pole towering straight up like some support structure for an invisible miniature suspension bridge out of the dead man's forehead.

"You have one thing right in that piece of shit you call a brain. He was flirting with me," she went on without once turning her head towards the soldier's body. "And I let him because if I gave him the cold shoulder he would have abandoned us. Couldn't you see? Are your eyes that shut off to the world?"

"I should have paid more heed."

"Give me a break," she said. Then she tripped over a protruding root, perhaps the same one he had tripped over earlier, but he grabbed her around the waist to keep her from falling. As soon as she regained her balance, she elbowed him sharply in the side. After a long silence her expression softened. "Perhaps it was wrong of me to flirt given what had just happened between us, but you can't deny he *would* have been an asset. Especially given the circumstances. That is, if he didn't turn out to be a complete animal."

When they got back to the shack Anderson opened the door and helped her across the threshold. She accepted his aid and allowed him to guide her to a chair. As he cleansed the two deep gashes on her legs with tap water and a piece of cloth torn from his shirt, she told him what had happened the night he abandoned them, her eyes taking on the same dead metallic gray of the sky outside.

"We heard a noise," she said. She closed her eyes and her voice went quiet and slow as though she were enjoying for a moment the sensation of hovering outside of her body and listening to herself as she spoke. "He got up and walked into the woods. Then I heard him shout like he was in danger and I followed him. When I caught up to him all I could see was his face in the light of the moon. Everything else was black as though the world was absorbing all light. He looked so pure and innocent. I asked him what had happened and he grabbed my arm and squeezed it as though he were in need of some kind of affection or support. He said he had heard an animal and had followed it for a short distance and then tripped. That was when he had shouted. I then took his hand and guided him back to the fire hearth. When we got there we stayed up for a few minutes talking. He said something about the world closing in on itself and how everyone was become smaller relative to the cosmos and how he needed something or someone to save him from the war."

He didn't say anything. It seemed that silence was the only form of tenderness he could offer. She opened her eyes and Anderson caressed her face with the warm cloth, watching as the beads of water gathered in small rings on her forehead and then fell like pearls from an unstrung necklace to the floor.

"When I stood up to go to my sleeping bag and join you he touched my arm in a more pure and sincere way than I had ever been touched, yet for some reason it seemed repugnant, as though by acknowledging it in any way I was automatically granting him some form of foothold in my life, and therefore opening myself to his manipulation and domination."

She stopped talking, allowing Anderson to admire the smooth contours of her face as she tried to gather herself to continue. "When I saw that you were gone I thought you must have just walked away for a moment. I waited for you to come back, not daring to go and tell the soldier that you had disappeared. Then everything went blank. The next thing I knew I was awake in some forest with my feet and hands tied up. For hours I was alone. Then, just as it started to get dark, the soldier came back. He didn't say anything. All he did was untie my feet and point a gun to my back. We went like that, him behind me, completely silent and jabbing me with the gun every few minutes to make me walk faster."

Again she stopped, but this time Anderson knew she would not start up again. Her face seemed to gain weight, precluding the possibility of speech by virtue of its very gravity. Whatever else had happened to her she wasn't going to share with him, at least not now, and likely not ever because they would certainly be finished together once they found safety across the border. He could see it in her eyes. It was as though they had receded into her body and healed over to bare flesh and there was nothing more to be had or said and that by even asking her what had happened he would be risking further anger and recriminations by ignoring the invisible cue she had laid out before him.

What the soldier had done to her behind the shack was something his imagination did not want to encounter. His mind moved in dark Rubenesque brush strokes, painting one macabre scenario after another like stark canvases rife with blood-spent annihilation hanging in some ancient mausoleum or torture chamber. He imagined that the soldier had taken her up to the shack and tried to rape her or actually and more likely did rape her. He imagined the man's face as he pulled a long slender blade out of his pants and brandished it in her face, the silvery surface winking in the light as she screamed for help. He imagined other things, more primal and abstract, pure forms of violence rather than violence itself, the very images that might have flowed through the soldier's mind, egging him on from some dark and etheric world whose substance was a mere whisper in the darkness of our own, as he thrust himself at her with all his savage might.

Anna coughed and he set his hand silently on her neck. She closed her eyes, clearly and openly enduring a great pain. He thought of the soldier's dead body. Had Anna actually killed him by thrusting the pole through his forehead, or was a third party involved? He yearned to know what the soldier had done to her and how he had come to die like that. It was a strange irony that in all his years of being a journalist the police always gave him a complete and clinical account of everything that happened on any crime scene to any complete stranger but now that such a thing had happened to Anna he would be forever banned from possessing such knowledge. Perhaps she might tell someone else some day, a random stranger sitting on a park bench some Sunday afternoon, but never him. That was what it meant to be or have once been one's lover. To give unconditional support while knowing it was impossible to have an equally unconditional access to the truth. In his heart he knew what probably had happened and to ask her to repeat the details was a form of cruelty he just wasn't capable of.

"It's cold here," she said faintly. She dug her fingers lightly into the flesh of his arm. "What's going to happen now?" She closed her eyes and fell asleep almost immediately.

Outside the rain had stopped and the leaves on the trees glowed with a rare depth and saturation of color as though transplanted from a world of dream. A heron flew by, dipping slightly in a gust of wind, and some unnamed bird of prey followed a tight descending spiral over an abandoned farmhouse as though stalking an unseen snake or rodent. Anderson watched the bird, wondering how it was possible that he had gone on living for so long without killing himself. He felt that moment like little more than the sum of all those things people had always hated about him, or rather, those things that he suspected people hated about him yet were always too kind to say anything about. Inside there was nothing but shame and once that was peeled away there was nothing. Somewhere at sometime the process of him becoming the asshole she had said he was had all started and somehow he failed to see what was happening early enough to nip it in the bud because of this emotional blindness then went off track. People all started equally as people and then for one reason or another dried up inside or flowered and finally became something or nothing, depending. But why they dried up was always because of something that was already there before they were born and had no control over. No one could really be held responsible for what they had become and there really was no beginning as there was always something before that stood there shaping the beginning and because of this had to have a beginning of its own. Scientists looked for the beginning of all things in some cathartic and pseudo-religious event like the big bang, just trying to satisfy their unconscious urge to ground their existence in something tangible and concrete. But if you were an asshole nobody ever wanted to know why you were an asshole and what series of events had made you into one and in the end it was impossible to step outside of life and assign such definite points to such vague and subjective things anyway. If you were beaten up by someone when you were little it was always by someone who was beaten up by someone else and if you went back far enough back in time you lost all track and whatever prime mover bully there was supposed to be at the end of the chain – maybe some Cro-Magnon that started it all by throwing sand at some Neanderthal – was never really there anyway.

It was almost dark. A distant church bell struck, reminding Anderson of those things that still needed to be done and that he and Anna were not alone in the world. He felt something like a mirage of comfort as he looked at her figure lying beside him, her fingers still clinging loosely to his wrist. It was only in others that his life gained any sense of meaning or solid ground. The windows frosted over with condensed humidity and the world outside took on an even more dreamlike appearance. He pulled Anna even closer and then closed his eyes as he listened to the rhythm of her beating heart. He thought he could smell something like rose blossoms and tar mingling with the cold humid air but the illusion quickly vanished.

Part III

135

I

Anderson held Anna's hand as much as she allowed him to as they walked down the base of the mountain towards Virovitica, crossing first a narrow wooden bridge that itself crossed a small brook. Beneath the surface of the water they could see the outlines of slithering dark shapes, long and thin like fish or eels, vanish and reappear, apparently at their will, from behind the rounded silver rocks that lined the riverbed beneath them. Anderson inhaled deeply and surveyed the landscape around them. Trees, rocks, birds, and grass: everything looked as it always had before he had abandoned Anna. Nothing had happened to change anything in the world. But deep inside himself he knew this was untrue, and nothing with her would ever be the same. That much in the universe had changed and would never go back to being what it was before.

They crossed a large open field, bedded with tall swaying cat tails, the rounded tops of which were coated with a thin layer of hoarfrost. You can cross the same waters twice, but other waters will pass over you, he recalled the loosely translated quote of Hericlitus. If *waters* were the variable elements in life then the point in the river you crossed was the relationship you had with others, which in its core was immutable, but on the surface always appeared different. Places changed, careers changed, children were born and relatives died, but you were always dealing with essentially the same problems over and over again. This was at odds with the more popular interpretation of the lines that everything was always in flux and that when you met up with an old friend years later everything would be different. He repeated the maxim in his head several times before it eventually gave way to his memory of the incoherent hissing of rain when he first found Anna lying on the ground beside the dead soldier.

They continued across the field and down towards a much heavier wooden footbridge than the one they had just crossed. Situated between the base of a mountain and the foot of a plain, the bridge looked like it could have once been the center of a great battle. About fifty meters in front of it a U-shaped grove of laurel trees towered from the ground, and in the center of this grove a slender wooden well rose from the ground. Looming on the side of the path and ten meters from the head of the bridge was a tall sign depicting the silhouette of a camera with a deep red X slashed through it.

"Why would they want to ban photographs?" Anna said in a way that sounded more British than American. "There must have been some secret military base somewhere around. I've never seen a sign like that outside of an art gallery or some nocturnal animal house in a zoo."

When they reached the edge of the bridge they slowed their pace, setting one foot deliberately ahead of the other in a stiff pattern of movement that would have seemed to any onlooker more like a performance by a mime artist than any real effort to move forward. Anna's hair blew around her face in small rivulets and tangles that gathered, broke apart, and then reformed into completely new rivulets and tangles in a beautiful dance of glittering auburn hair and peach-white skin. A large and awkward bird flew overhead and then disappeared under the bridge. Anna coughed weakly and for a moment the world split in half and Anderson felt like two people, the noble and thoughtful person that had first met her, and the petty and selfish man that had recently abandoned her in search of whatever false deity could bring on the flowering of his independence. Neither was the current Anderson, yet each one had its role in the present moment and all the feelings and doubts that flowed between him and the woman walking beside him.

"I'm sorry," he said, not really knowing which part of him was speaking.

Anna kept looking ahead in a way that was neither detached nor involved. When they reached the other side of the bridge she turned to him and narrowed her eyes like a woman in a movie putting on a face that was both sexy and astute. Then she looked away. He thought he heard the echo of fighter planes roaring overhead as he cleared his throat like a man about to make an important speech.

"When I first found you," he said, "I thought anything I said would be ridiculous in light of what happened and that for me to even ask or probe any further or conversely for me to bow down to your feet and beg forgiveness would only be an empty gesture and the fact I came back to get you was enough to prove that I was sorry. I know you probably hate me now and will never forgive me."

Anna remained suspended in a state of ambiguous silence. Was it some kind of tacit approval of what he had just said, or just a sign of her utter negation of him?

"I had a terrifying experience," he continued, being careful not to end his statement with the words "as well" to make sure she didn't think he was trying to trivialize what had happened to her. Then he went on to tell her about the village in which everyone apparently had been slaughtered. "A man I met who lived alone in the woods said that a solider was responsible for the massacre, but I wasn't sure if he was telling the truth or if it really was the same man..."

"I have heard as much as I want to," she said resignedly. She looked into his eyes and he felt a soft feeling as though she were at once beside him and within him. "When the soldier left me alone outside the shack a realization came over me that what you did in abandoning me and what he was then doing to me and what I did to you in deceiving you for almost a year were all forms of the same thing. In a way I started to feel sorry for him. He became to me a lost and misguided child desperately following the call of some inner demon. And after that I was no longer afraid of him. I saw that no matter how dangerous he seemed that I was always in control."

He suddenly felt as though he were confronting a person he didn't know, someone whose views he found startling and repugnant.

"You're afraid of what I'm saying," she said.

"No," he said.

"Yes you are." She stopped and looked into his eyes in the same way she always did before the affair. He felt at ease, but he did not believe her worlds and wondered if it was just some rationalization to ease her trauma or likewise ease his sense of guilt to avoid complications until they crossed the border to safety. It was something in her he knew too well, something that ultimately stemmed from all the things about her that had drawn him to her in the first place. Hers was a beauty of strength and abundance that always denied any weakness and always held something in reserve.

"After he first lunged at me with the pole I managed to distract him for long enough to grab it away. Then he came at me again and I closed my eyes and thrust it towards him as hard as I could. And you saw what happened. After that I was in such shock I just sat there on the ground shivering for so long I lost all track of time. I don't even want to remember what thoughts flew through my mind before you found me. It was a strange cold feeling that all human relationships were tainted, corrupt and selfish."

Anderson put his arm around her to comfort her and make her feel that that their relationship was unique and subject to different laws than any other but she did not allow him to touch her for long.

"Do you think I would have had the affair if I hadn't felt abandoned? When I was a girl my violin teacher always used to tell me all these horrible stories about Debussy. He abandoned his wife to compose *La Mer* by the seaside while she sank into depression and ultimately killed herself. My teacher used to tell me how awful everyone thought he was and how only thirteen people showed up at his funeral. She used to tell me this story when I felt like nobody liked me, and the world was a dreadful place. You know the way you get when you're a teenager. It was her way of saying that no matter what people thought of Debussy they were wrong because he was obviously a good person as evidenced by the beautiful piano works he left behind."

There was a smell like wet hay in the air that reminded Anderson of a time he had spent on a farm working one summer when he was still in grade school, a time when he became convinced he could tell the time of day by reading the expressions on people's faces or the length and shading of the shadows cast by trees on the edges of the cornfield.

"But goodness doesn't necessarily follow from beauty," he said.

"That's precisely what I am trying to say. I thought she was wrong and what the Debussy story told me was how for everything beautiful to exist there had to be something equally ugly or evil to help it come into existence. He was selfish and probably enjoyed watching his wife suffer, logging the subtle nuances of her depression and using them as inspiration for *Claire de Lune* or

Les Arabesques." She paused and took a deep breath and then continued in the tone of an orator. It was a trait he always admired in her, the ability to extract the profound and grandiose from the commonplace or even treacherous. "For all beauty to come into existence, something must suffer."

"And for any good action, there must always be a selfish desire lurking somewhere behind," he said, reflecting into words what he guessed she was thinking.

"The way I see it the artist sucks life dry of its feeling and beauty and spits it out as some higher form of creation just so he can etch himself a permanent position in history."

"And what would you say about the lover?" he asked. "What does he do?"

"The lover? I'm not sure. But, maybe all lovers are ultimately no different than artists, regardless of their intentions. Whether he is a Casanova or a Young Werther, he is ultimately fulfilling his own selfish needs and thus acting out of self preservation."

"But if it helps *the other*, then how is it selfish? And how can you say Debussy was just selfish and not instead enslaved by some self destructive desire to create beauty, even at the expense of his own well being?"

"Now," she whispered. "*Now*, you are finally understanding me. Can't you see that I'm just trying to find some way to forgive you?"

The ground ahead of them was covered with a thin layer of snow. In some areas, individual blades of grass had risen through the smooth white sheet like nascent green shoots sprouting from an ocean of sand, while in other places clusters of weeds had pushed much larger holes through the snow, giving the earth a rough and mottled appearance like the coat of a snow leopard.

"You once told me that you became a violinist out of excess," he said, remembering the sight of her supple red lips moving in the light of an overhanging sodium vapor streetlight as they walked home one dry August night, the sound of crickets coursing through the air like strange African rhythm instruments. A satellite winked in the night sky before vanishing behind an unseen cloud. He had been out hopping the local bars for the first time in several months and all the pieces of his life seemed to have suddenly fallen together. He felt warm inside like all his problems had been solved and he wondered why he had avoided alcohol and nightlife for so long in the first place, although in the back of his mind he knew it was to help him save money while he was completing the year-abroad requirement of his journalism program. After a few months of abstinence he started feeling *the same* all the time and forgot what it was like to feel any other way. During periods of excess there was always the excitement of the ups and downs: the long dull afternoons followed by the first few glasses of wine or Pilsner that would always lift him back into a state of surrogate normality; the lights in his head would finally switch back on and all would once again be bliss.

"Perhaps other people become artists or fall in love out of *lack*," he finally replied. "Maybe Debussy felt small and insignificant and that the only way his life had any meaning was if he created something beautiful."

Anna looked at him, her lips shining the way they had that same night under the streetlight. Then she spoke. "When I was a young woman I always thought all musicians were uptight and I approached my lessons and performances with love and excess rather than the desire to hone and whittle myself into the societal sculpture for public viewing I then believed orchestras represented.

But that feeling of recklessness is now gone and I can see quite clearly there will be no *arabesques* to come from all this and we are best off parting ways."

Anderson followed the shape of a mountain on the horizon. When he looked back at her the connections between art, love, selfishness, and evil had suddenly grayed and he wondered if what they had been saying really made any sense at all or if they were just following a vague and fanciful train of thought only disguised as something deep and profound in order to keep their minds off whatever hurt and anger was still simmering between them.

"Yes," he said. "I think I understand." He looked away again, not really sure if he had understood anything she had said. A great distance opened up between them and they both fell silent. There was a sudden motion in the grass beside him. Anderson turned and looked, expecting to see some small animal like a rodent or snake, but there was nothing. He turned back to Anna and took her hand in the way a young man might do at a first dance. She let him touch it for a moment before pulling it away sharply.

When they reached the outskirts of Virovitica a pale blanket of smoke had settled over the highest rooftops and steeples, suggesting that a fire had just occurred or was still ongoing. The air had a sharp sulfurous smell and the streets were empty as though they had been evacuated in an organized and orderly fashion. Two blocks further in from the perimeter, beside a small stone church in the doorway of which stood a short man wearing a red sun hat, the smoke had seemed to clear, although Anderson wasn't sure if this was only because they had penetrated deeper into the village to an area that was completely enveloped by the smoke, and that their nose and eyes had just gotten used to it. The man with the red hat turned abruptly, as though fearing he had been spotted by someone he was hiding from, and then disappeared inside the church.

They continued down a narrow alleyway, extending into the depths of a residential neighborhood several blocks away, until they reached an intersection beyond which rose the minarets and domes of an ornate building that looked like the work of Moorish invaders from centuries before. When they crossed the street Anderson became aware once more of the acrid sulfurous smell, although this time it was more intense than before.

"Shall we find a place to stay?" Anna asked in the tone of a firm suggestion rather than a question.

"We have to get you to a hospital."

"No. I will be fine," she said. She had a calm look in her eyes that made him think for a moment that she really was fine and that what had happened with the soldier was not anywhere near as serious as it could have been. But deep inside he knew she was just acting this way and that she couldn't really be fine at all.

"I know you can't be," he said. "But if what you really want is a place to sleep, then we can find a hotel."

An hour later, after walking around the village in search of a bed and breakfast, they finally checked into a small bed and breakfast that offered single rooms with a private shower and a television. Outside their window an empty fountain gushed in glittering columns of water and leaning against its white-painted cement rim was a small rusted tricycle enveloped by the shadow of a statue of Neptune holding a golden trident. Behind the fountain stood a wire fence on top of which were perched a row of pigeons, each bird fatuously bobbing its head back and forth as though pecking away at an invisible wall. Anderson turned up the heat and undressed. They showered separately, and for a moment they crossed paths outside the bathroom door while both were still naked and then she showered herself, leaving the door wide open. She did not look at him once as he smoothed a soft sponge over her unyielding body as the water splashed and steamed over her, being sure not to press too hard as her hand passed over the many tiny bruises on her legs and hips. As he dressed he watched himself in the full-length mirror by the bed, hardly recognizing the gaunt and pale figure that stood there before him. The walls of the room were covered in faded wallpaper with what he thought was a Rococo or Baroque design, composed of interlocking cascades of pink and green vines and flowers. When the sun finally set and only a pink light remained on the horizon, in full view from the window, he closed the dusty green curtains and flicked the light switch. Anna was already in bed. He took off his clothes and stretched out beside her.

II

A golden light flowed into the room as Anderson opened the curtains and looked out onto the street, this same golden light illuminating the figure of a man holding a basket of corn, his back hunched over slightly to his left, the weight of the basket almost too great for him to bear. Anderson closed the curtains and turned around. Anna was still asleep with only the top half of her face now visible, a radiant patch of white skin and hair winking in the morning light from under the warm cradle of her blanket. He knelt down beside her. The room had the feel of a gothic chapel, replete with soaring arches and cavernous spaces, a place where thoughts and feeling floated as freely as rays of light filtering through a wall of stained glass windows. Anna rolled over and opened her eyes. Her expression was that of a child just awoken from a pleasant dream into a world that seems unfamiliar and misplaced. He leaned over and caressed her face. She tightened her eyelids and then loosened them again before closing them completely as though he was not even there before her. Then she nudged her face into the pillow.

"You were so troubled yesterday," she spoke into the pillow before pushing it away. "You must feel that everything that happened was your fault." She paused and looked away from him, as though in shame. "So I want you to know the truth before you torture yourself anymore," she said with gaining wakefulness that quickly turned to clarity. "I killed him before he could rape me."

He looked into her eyes, gleaming and blue, and said nothing. He wondered if she was only lying to him to make him feel better.

He shrugged his shoulders and leaned over to kiss her. Her hair had the perfumed smell of wet leaves and forest floor. He cupped his hand over her breast and let his body crumple into hers.

"What are we going to do when we get to Hungary?" she asked, her eyes penetrating into him as though searching for a solution to a question she had not asked, an answer to which did not exist.

"Maybe we should take the first plane out," he answered.

A cat screeched from somewhere far and distant and from even further in the distance came the sound of shouting. Although he had only been to Budapest twice, it had somehow come to signify for him *being* in its most elevated and abstract sense. Countless times he had walked down *Andrássy ut* watching the leaves of the overhanging trees blowing in the wind while hurried Ladas sped to their unknown destinations on the road beside him. In his memory these moments held the same exalted a position as the woman in the apartment carried away in an ambulance or the book he was trying to write in his recurring dreams. He would sit for hours on park benches in Budapest reflecting on nothing but the world around him. While in most other places he always felt busied and annoyed by the outside world, the small cafés along the Danube always brought upon him a peace of mind where stasis and beauty seemed to flow from every point and every moment was ripe with expression and the world drew him in rather than drove him away. Even the Hungarian language held a special signature for this state of becoming where one felt immediately transposed into the dynamic between stasis and change. There was a special ending for adjectives or nouns that were being changed by the agent of the verb. It was a case devoted entirely to *becoming*. *Tegye boldoggá a családát* meant make your family happy, where *boldog* was happy and *boldoggá* was modified to imply a change in the family from a state of non-happiness to one of happiness. And then there was the word "való", without equivalent in English. It was a word that drew back to the origin or essence of a thing, its birthplace, its function, its very "being" in the most primal and abstract sense of the word. In only a matter of hours they would be in Barcs and soon after that on a train surging through the Hungarian countryside to Budapest. Trips always fascinated him: train trips, boat trips, and even bus trips. And "trip" to him meant "city". What was a city but a massive agglomeration of trips and treks by inhabitants? To cross from one point to another in a world composed of nothing but intersecting routes and people, all themselves embarking on their own small voyages or journeys. Each trip was a connection of points and hence a unique synthesis of roads and experiences similar to a complex thought or feeling, all pointing towards the word "city".

When they checked out of the hotel it was already midday. As they walked down the main street of the village, lined with lush green trees and gray stone walls, Anderson sensed the fragments of his life had only just begun to fall back together again like pieces of a scattered jigsaw puzzle. But how long would this take and how long would the new and ensuing form last? When he got back to New York and all the dust had settled, or just as likely blew completely asunder, would he be "the writer who no longer has anything to say and becomes consumed by his own indolence" or "the man whose love of life flows outwards towards others" or "the man who has run away from dark black funnel clouds in his dreams for several years only to one day confront the tornado in all its savage beauty in one final cathartic dream and find that he is in fact its master"? These were questions he could not yet answer. All he knew was that in the wealth of Anna's provisional forgiveness it was his duty to search for in the eyes and faces of others the same generosity that she had shown him. While before they left Pozega a crowd of people constituted an impersonal entity and he would always shut himself off from the world of individual expressions, now he saw that each person's face was a secret well from the depths of which could be drawn countless lessons for existence.

"At the end of a relationship the lover becomes all that he or she lacks and doesn't provide the other," Anna said as they walked past a strange building with a rounded wooden roof that looked as though it was once a mill or granary. "When I was unfaithful to you, *he* was all those things I wished you were, but when I was alone on the mountain I realized that you were also those things, but I had only allowed myself to become blinded to you. I had become deadened to those things in you I had always loved. I started looking for those same qualities in someone else when it was really my own *lack* that had closed my eyes to you and prevented me from seeing you as you really were."

Anderson turned his gaze down the road in the direction of what looked like a Croatian military base. They were safely outside of Serbian territory at last. He felt translucent, almost colorless, as though he was but a sum of all that came to him from outside. Yet it was a feeling that seemed perfectly natural, as though all of creation was only defined by what it wasn't – and hence by its imprint in the world around it - instead of what it actually was. A truck roofed by a canvas canopy turned into a lane and drove inside a fenced-off compound. Weren't he always just craving for the end of things? Or was it rather their beginning? Weren't all black holes only condensed stars which one day might explode in a vast symphony of beauty and forgetfulness? Penis. Flute. Orpheus. Nihlos. Words of a languid poet waiting to be consumed by something much greater and more beautiful than himself. Even in that profoundly curved tulip-shaped glass of Richebourg, wasn't he just longing to lose himself in its smoke and ruby corridors, stained with purple light like a great robe of nothingness? To vanish into

Anna's flesh and very being was to become more than anyone ever could be alone; maybe this was why ancient religions had always linked destruction and creation.

When he emerged from his reverie he noticed Anna was watching him as though reading his thoughts like an invisible form of Braille. She was just about to say something when a small lime-colored Volkswagen sped past her, its trail of wind blowing her hair across her forehead. When her hair had settled a much more serious expression had crystallized on her face. He turned away from her and looked straight ahead. The sun reflected off a shiny black mirage of its own making and the road was clear and empty.

Later that afternoon they crossed a great white plain, covered with short fat bushes no higher than his shin, and this white plain rose and fell in gentle inclines but was strangely bereft of any sign of life. The sky was a crisp blue, so deep and alive that it evoked thoughts of Egyptian deities. How beautiful was the silence that such a space afforded them. It reminded him of a time a year after he had married Anna during which nothingness became their most common form of communication. Whenever he felt like saying something important, his thoughts would always present themselves as something incomplete that required far more time and development before they could be uttered and understood and to attempt to voice them any sooner would have only created misunderstandings and poison the air between them. So for an entire winter he said only the bare minimum to her – only simple orders, instructions, or requests that had to be vocalized. "Pass the salt please", or "I'll do the dishes" was enough, a kind of secret language they both understood. What he found the strangest was that during this period their lovemaking was more intense than it ever had been and their relationship shared a level of affection it never had before.

At the end of the plain a river gurgled and on the other side of this river and further over the crest of a small hill a small town lay in a cradle of parkland, the green areas cut into small segments by a series of interlocking canals. The air was alive with an alpine freshness and there was a calm eccentricity dwelling in the eyes of the people. Without looking at the road signs he had a feeling they were near the border.

"This place seems so forlorn...so hidden or tucked away," Anna said. They stopped beneath a massive oak tree, even its shadow towering over the diminutive church beside it. "It's almost as if its very essence is to remain stolen from the world, a place devoid of action or participation with anything outside itself."

"As though participation in the world is necessarily a good thing..." Anderson replied.

"I wasn't saying it was or it wasn't. I was just making an observation. Maybe being *away* from things is a form of purity or goodness." She emphasized the word "away" by drawing it out in a long, almost musical fashion, and Anderson wondered if this was her way of torturing him, by subtly reminding him that she would never be his again and that everything they had shared was only a memory and what they were sharing now was just a pallid reenactment of this thing, once so strong and bountiful, that had existed between them.

III

When they reached the Hungarian border the guard examined their passports and asked them many questions such as how long they intended to stay and if they had proof they would be leaving and not trying to find work, how much money they were carrying and what were their respective occupations. The guard's face then became even more serious than it had been and he asked them if they had heard of *Operation Otkos* or that there had been a massacre at Vukovar and they said they had not. After what seemed like an hour of questions punctuated by several lengthy occasions during which the guard went into the other room to speak to his colleague in Hungarian, they were finally granted passage into Barcs. It was a small village, the central business area of which was dominated by a dilapidated train station, its unusual slanted wooden roof painted blue as though to mirror the sky and the walls built from white stone blocks, now smoothed around the edges by years of wear. The station was empty except for a man seated in the ticket booth and a taller older man feeding pigeons by a wastebasket from a brown paper bag. The old man repeated some phrase over and over again to the pigeons and took little note of Anderson as he walked up to the ticket officer and asked in English for two one-way tickets to Budapest. The man behind the counter accepted his money in silence and handed him the change. A young girl carrying a school bag walked by in quick choppy steps as though late for a class but not worried enough to break into a run. She was dressed in a dark blue and white dress adorned at the top with a sailor's collar, her straight brown hair falling to her shoulders like a silky chestnut waterfall. The train arrived ten minutes later. Anderson took Anna's hand and helped her on board. The cars were divided into three small sections, each with several sets of modern upholstered seats facing one another. The train idled for ten minutes before a whistle blew from somewhere outside, prompting a crowd of people to come as if from nowhere to fill the cabin to capacity.

At times the trip to Budapest seemed longer than the entire journey from Pozega. They passed through a precipitous mountainous area on the far end of which lay equidistant expanses of barren fields separated by tall stone fences that stretched off into the distance, eventually becoming little more than long gray lines. It seemed they stopped at each and every village they passed, letting off exactly as many people as came on to replace them. By the time they got to Budapest it was already well past sundown, but the pinkish light on the horizon was just enough to cast a silvery halo around the buildings, seeming to lift the stone edges from the blackness surrounding them in some form of visual embossing.

As soon as they stepped off the train Anderson felt accosted by a world of pure image. A small flock of pigeons feeding on scraps of candy bars and small pieces of wrapping paper flew off as though part of a giant flower blooming forth in a torrent of thudding wings and pink-gray feathers, connected by a set of invisible wires controlling each bird in the same way a person could control the individual limbs of his body with the network of nerves inside. A soft light filtered through the station's dirtied glass ceiling. They walked along the platform, dodging passengers who were still disembarking, moving in slow deliberate steps until they reached the main entrance.

Outside the streets seemed strangely alive for the time of day. Couples dressed in dark wool coats and autumn hats rushed by as though late for a reservation at some upscale restaurant. A man holding a small violin stepped up to Anderson and tipped his hat before receding into the crowd, possibly to go and repeat this gesture to someone else, equally unknown to him. A few pigeons landed on the street corner and Anderson mused over the chances they were part of the same flock that flew off a moment before from the train station. There was a scent of something like freshly baked bread in the air and he was seized by a feeling that life – even time in its most real and tangible sense – was little more than a trick of some indifferent God, a house of cards that could collapse at any minute to reveal an underlying level of existence which was deeper, darker, and more primordial than the world he had always known yet lacked all forms of extension or temporality and was for this reason closer to this God. Every object before him – the wires on the power lines, the signs lining the railway, the white birch trees standing starkly in the distance – stood as mocking reminders that all of "this" was but an illusion and was not the world from which he had been born. "I am not of this world," he thought, repeating in his head the immortal lines of Rimbaud.

"What are we going to do now?" Anna asked with her trademark naivety. Yet he sensed her question was far more serious, loaded with a multitude of meanings. Now that they were back in *the world of men* what would they do?

"We can go get something to eat," he said, ignoring the perceived more serious side of her question.

She said absolutely nothing as she lifted her arm and draped it around Anderson's shoulder in a way that seemed like a mockery of how lovers walk, rather than showing any sincere sign of affection. Yet in its attempted irony, it had to be taken as a positive thing, a sign that she was approaching life with new found levity and had possibly even begun the process of putting the past behind her.

They made their way down a broad boulevard, lined with a series of uneventful shops, each with a sale of some sort advertised in the window. A torrent of thoughts roared through him. Where was the woman who had been carted off to hospital years before? Since witnessing the massacre he had begun to feel his life couldn't go on without this knowledge. And his book of dreams (or was it really just a dream of a book?) Was it well received? Was it even written yet? Was he a Prospero or a Falstaff? Would he have to dream on and on through countless bad reviews only to wake up sweating in bed knowing it was all a dream but also knowing this dream had some higher meaning that had hitherto remained elusive to him? He looked over at Anna and everything came to him in a *blossoming forth* of feeling and inner visions. A car rushed by, but the sound and fumes from its blaring engine had no effect on him. Anna was a being fallen from the wall of the Sistine chapel, she was the scent of a hot summer evening on top of a hill overlooking a great valley while the starry firmament glittered and pulsed in the sky above, she was the dying of the light and the light itself. Through her he could see the world. Through her he could gain the strength to solve his great internal puzzle. The world was two or more and was never one, unless this one was in fact the unification of all rather than its atomization: thus was salvation in the face of the other in all her vastness and complexity, resolved or unresolved, fit or not fit, together in the only way it could ever be.

They approached a woman who was standing alone on the sidewalk starring into space and shouting out at some invisible lover. Wasn't "the other" always invisible? She wore a thick down coat that looked far too warm for the season, and carried a small gift in her hand, shaking it as though she had just offered it to someone who had summarily refused it, thus insulting her. A small dog with dirty white fur ran leapt out of a restaurant and barked at the woman. She turned around and hurled the gift at it, but it dodged the attack and quickly darted across the street, vanishing behind a silvery tour bus as it passed. Anderson broke out laughing. Why had the dog been in the restaurant to begin with? Yet this thought gave way to a cascade of other thoughts, each of which was equally detached and irrelevant. Would he order salad or bean broth? What was the Forint relative to the pound? Who was winning the World Series and had it even started yet?

They strolled into the shadow of a brown apartment building, tall glass windows gleaming on every floor. The sound of cello rumbled from a window on the third floor. The bass was deep and full, silky and rounded, but also detailed, filling the air with a warm and comforting feeling the likes of which he had not felt since before he first came to Yugoslavia. But then a more troubling thought came over him. Maybe the musicians were people more kindred to Anna than he was and if she ever met them or anyone like them they would latch onto her and adore her for her beauty and emotional "roundness" in a way that would forever exclude him. When he looked over to gauge Anna's reaction to the music, she had a distant expression on her face like someone absorbed in a book. A cat ran in front of them and stopped, as though to inspect them, before disappearing behind a garbage can. He returned his glance to the apartment building and it suddenly looked different, more sinister. Its windows were eyes and a mouth and its walls were the cold and clinical armor of a heartless stone giant. He shuddered inside at the thought of Anna sitting inside talking about music with people he had never met and never wanted to meet. It was something that he didn't want to happen yet would no doubt happen over and over again in countless other forms and guises throughout his life. It was all that stuff that leaked in from outside or corroded you from within and destroyed your attempts to get closer to someone. It was people like the soldier and the Frenchman – men he still preferred not to mention by name out of some form of condescension. But wasn't he giving them a special elevated status by refusing to name them? Were they not, then, like Yahweh? And the way they made him feel and the way his jealousy only made her want to move further away from him and start seeing the Frenchman in the first place...

A whistle blew in the distance and he noticed Ann was now smiling at him as though she had been secretly watching him all along while he was looking across at the apartment building. Who were those people playing the cello and, even more importantly, what would he and Anna do when they got back to New York? What would happen now that he had saved her and her affair was over? What new forces would insinuate themselves into his life to try to keep her away from him? An ambulance drove by, its siren wailing slowly and deeply like a dying animal, as Anna grabbed his hand and squeezed it tightly, but he did not know why she did this and wondered if even she knew why.

"I guess we should try to get something to eat," she said.

Anderson nodded his head and followed her across the street and around a corner to a small restaurant adorned with two heavy iron lamps hanging from above the front entrance. He felt strangely vulnerable, as though he was standing alone in the midst of an impenetrable metal fortress, but one without doors, courtyards, or entranceways. A young man with a small bushy beard and a buckskin jacket grinned as he walked by. He was wearing tight black pants and had two identical jade earrings, one in each ear. He stopped and turned to Anderson, his light green eyes shining in the headlights of the passing cars.

"Score?" he asked. At first Anderson thought he was referring to a game or match of some kind.

"No…I mean I didn't see the game."

"Game?" The young man broke out laughing and walked away. "Horse doesn't kill you, it just slows you down." Then he barred his teeth in a way that was almost simian.

The man's heels clicked incessantly on the surface of the sidewalk as he walked away in the general direction of the river. Needle, Ass, Rilke: the three words hovered in Anderson's head like mad, disparate forms from another world. It was only on trying to figure out why these words in particular, and not three other words, appeared in his head that he realized what the man had meant by "horse".

The lights of the city darkened and a deep orange yellow floodlight turned on from the other side of the Danube, illuminating the Chain Bridge and the Fisherman's Bastion, its tall narrow spires and square battlements rising majestically from the water. A woman leaned out from a window in a modern style apartment building and shook the dust out of a carpet. Across the street a man walked into a fabric store, rolls of exotic materials with silver and gold embroidery on display in the main window. "Szovetek," the sign read. Anderson wondered if the name had anything to do with the former Soviet Union and if it did whether the Hungarians, known to detest the Russians, held a grudge against the shop owner for not changing the name when the Iron Curtain came down. Anna was staring ahead, her eyes trained on the face of a small boy with short blond hair. The boy stopped in front of a French bistro and pointed, turning to a young woman wearing a purple jogging suit who looked like she could have been his sister. The woman nodded her head and grabbed the boy's hand, escorting him through the varnished oak doors into the restaurant.

"This looks good," said Anna. She pressed her hand against the door and leaned forward, allowing her weight to push it open. He followed her in and they sat directly across from one another at a small wooden table lit in the center by a dull yellow candle flame. The waiter came by and set two menus on the table before darting off into the kitchen as though he had just been called away on a secret rescue mission. Was there a fire in the kitchen? Would the food take longer than it was worth waiting for? Had a phone been ringing that had somehow remained unheard to him?

Anderson picked up his fork and held it up in the light, turning it this way and that to try and see if he could create reflections on its smooth metal palm. He set the fork down and exhaled. He knew it would not be long before they were back in America and now all he was sure of was that he wasn't sure he wanted to go back or even take one step further in any direction whether abstractly or concretely. His mind receded into a world in which he was standing on a New York street corner at Christmas watching all the crowds walk by as they ignited the world with their elegant shopping bags and pale rosy cheeks. Did he really miss all those lights and tall wavering glass and concrete forms stretching upwards to the dark fathomless sky with all the trains and cars rushing off like sinister caravans into the turnpikes and arteries leading to the "mad towns of the east" as Allen Ginsberg had once called them? Was man really falling away from God and was the world frozen in its own darkness, spinning on a cold leaden axis towards a perilous yet somehow utterly meaningless end or did all the small and incoherent unities in the world make up for all this and in their entirety comprise something even greater than those

Gods that man once bowed down before? And more tangibly, or perhaps even less, would she ever forgive him, or he forgive her for what had happened the last several weeks or years between them? Anna grabbed his hand and squeezed it solidly as though to give him the reassurance she knew he needed but also knew she might never be able to give him again no matter how much she craved to. He looked at her without saying anything and drew his hand away. It seemed that everything that happened between them would forever be a dark, unfathomable mystery.